30% off Cosmetol(

Thank you for buying *Cosmetology Guru: The Essential Information You Need to Pass the First Time (and Nothing Else!)*. We know you'll pass your Cosmetology State Board Exam with flying colors once you've absorbed all the information in this compact, fluff-free guide.

Do you want to cement your knowledge and make sure you *really* understand it? Do you wish to feel reassured you can recall that knowledge under exam conditions – with the types of questions that will appear on the real exam?

Then look no further than **Cosmetology Guru Online** – the perfect complement to this book. When you buy **Cosmetology Guru Online**, you'll get:

- **Hundreds of practice questions**

- **Six simulated exams**

- **A condensed version of this book** – so you can learn on your preferred device whenever you have a spare moment.

Cosmetology Guru Online is compatible with computers, smartphones, and tablets, so you can access it however you please.

Visit www.cosmetologyguru.com and enter 30OFFNOW at checkout for 30% off.

If you have any questions or concerns before you buy, simply email contact@cosmetologyguru.com and we'll get back to you right away!

Cosmetology Guru:

The Essential Information You Need to Pass the First Time (and Nothing Else!)

2023-2024

By the Cosmetology Guru Team

COSMETOLOGY
—— GURU ——

Contents

About This Book

Cosmetology Guru: The Essential Information You Need to Pass the First Time (and Nothing Else!) is different from your regular Cosmetology exam study guide. Why? Because we haven't filled it with lots of unnecessary information – the type of information that'll take forever to learn and NEVER be on the exam. Instead, it contains only the information that's essential for passing. Nothing else!

In order to pass, however, we don't believe it's enough simply to read the information and hope for the best. You need to study in a way that suits you, in order to make sure you're able to retain the information and recall it at the key moment: during the exam itself. That's why the first section of this book outlines some tactics for figuring out your learning style, making the most of your study sessions, and approaching exam day fully prepared.

(It's also a good idea to put your new knowledge to the test with some online practice tests and simulated exams. Ours are the best when it comes to how realistic they are! Head to **www.cosmetologyguru.com** to see what's included, then enter **30OFFNOW** at checkout for 30% off.)

There's some other information about the Cosmetology exam and the role of the cosmetologist near the front of the book – just in case you need it. The rest of the book is devoted to teaching you the essential information for each concept. The breakdown of sections is, Scientific Concepts: 30%, Hair Care and Services: 40%, Skin Care and Services: 15%, and Nail Care and Services: 15%.

Who are we?

Cosmetology Guru consists of a team of cosmetology test prep experts who know what it takes to succeed the first time. Our study materials are consistently kept up-to-date, and they include everything you need to pass your written exams. We want to make test prep fast, efficient, and effective - and we're rooting for you to succeed in becoming a certified cosmetologist.

Let's get started!

Now that you know all about this book and why we created it, it's time to get started on the rest of it. Let's go!

Understanding the Role of a Cosmetologist

What Does a Cosmetologist Do?

A cosmetologist is a beauty professional who is licensed to provide various hair, skin, and nail services. There are different specialties that fall under each category, making it a broad field.

Full-time cosmetologists generally work 40-60 hours per week – and they spend that time doing more than just beautifying their clients. Along with cutting long locks, dying hair, giving facials, and painting nails, cosmetologists also undertake administrative duties and excel in proper sanitation techniques.

With a cosmetology license, you can fulfill roles such as:

- Hairdresser
- Nail technician
- Salon manager
- Cosmetology instructor
- Stylist
- and more!

Cosmetologists cannot be barbers without additional licensing. This means they cannot perform services such as shaving hair with a razor or straight razor without additional training.

What Are the Job Prospects for Cosmetologists?

Cosmetology, as a whole, is a job that is in high demand. It's been steadily growing in popularity ever since the early 2000s, and there are more jobs to fill than there are people to fill them.

The largest number of cosmetologists are working for personal care services, including hairdressing and beauty salons. Their next-largest employer is general merchandise stores. Health and personal care stores, or drug stores, are in third place, and the motion picture and video industries are the next.

Overall, the Bureau of Labor Statistics (BLS) predicts solid job prospects for new and current cosmetologists at least until 2030. In addition to the work created by rising demand, other jobs will open up as current workers retire or change careers.

How Much Do Cosmetologists Earn?

According to the BLS, the median hourly wage for hairdressers, hairstylists, and cosmetologists was $14.26 in May 2021 or $29,680 per year. The top 10 percent received at least $28.40 per hour, or $59,070 per year. Among cosmetologists in major industries, those working in the motion picture and video industries had the highest average pay - $36.86 per hour, or $76,670 yearly.

What are examples of future job opportunities for cosmetologists?

The BLS predicts that the number of jobs for cosmetologists will increase by 11 percent between 2021 and 2031: much faster than the average for all occupations. This growth will create an additional 93,800 openings per year through 2030. Americans have increased their demand for high-cost, specialty procedures such as hair straightening and coloring: a trend the BLS expects to continue. This growing market will increase the need for cosmetologists because these procedures are time-consuming.

About the Cosmetology Exam

What is the Cosmetology State Board Exam?

After completing your cosmetology program, you must appear for the state board exam to become a licensed cosmetologist.

In order to get your cosmetology license, you need to do the following:

- Complete the required number of hours at beauty school (the precise number of hours differs from state to state).
- Pass a practical exam (note: a small number of states don't have a practical exam).
- Pass a written exam.

Training and educational requirements vary depending on your chosen profession or where your studying or working. However, in the US, cosmetology is a regulated profession that requires all practitioners to be certified by state licensing boards.

This differs from state to state, but, generally speaking, the minimum age requirements are between 16-18. You will also need a high school diploma or GED, although some states accept a tenth-grade education.

Once you finally decide to take the exam, there are a few practical steps you can take before getting down to some intense studying:

1. Check with your local board – since each state that offers the state board exam has its own licensing requirements, you must first check how many hours of cosmetology

training you should complete before appearing for the exam.

2. Schedule your exam – it is always best to appear for the exam as soon as you complete your coursework. This way, the information will be fresh in your mind, and you will be able to understand the material you study easily. However, if your exam is delayed, you can still pass if you focus and revise your coursework.

3. Check the exam deadlines – you can get information regarding the exact deadline for the exam from your instructor. This is usually within six months after you have finished your course. However, exam deadlines can also depend on the state.

Now that you have done this, only the exam itself stands between you and your dream of becoming a licensed cosmetologist after graduating.

Written Exam

The following outlines the scope of content covered by the NIC National Cosmetology Theory Examination. The percentages represent the percentage of items from each domain. The examination consists of 110 items, 100 of which are weighted and contribute to the candidate's final score.

DOMAIN 1: SCIENTIFIC CONCEPTS (35%)

1A Scientific Concepts - Infection Control and Safety Practices

   1. Identify cause/transmission of diseases and infections
   2. Identify the purpose and differentiate among the categories of infection control
       a. Sanitation
       b. Disinfection
       c. Sterilization
   3. Recognize how cross-contamination occurs and how it can be prevented (e.g., single use and multi-use items)
   4. Apply blood exposure procedures
   5. Identify requirements of government agencies
       a. OSHA
       b. EPA

1B Scientific Concepts - Human Anatomy and Physiology

   1. Identify structure and functions of the:
       a. Hair and scalp
       b. Skin
       c. Nails
   2. Recognize signs and symptoms of conditions, disorders, and diseases related to:
       a. Hair and scalp
       b. Skin
       c. Nails

19

3. Identify muscles and joints and their functions related to:

    a. Head and face

    b. Arms and hands

    c. Legs and feet

4. Identify functions of:

    a. Nervous system

    b. Circulatory system

1C Scientific Concepts - Basic Chemistry used in Cosmetology

1. Recognize purpose and effects of ingredients

2. Recognize interactions between chemicals

3. Recognize chemical reactions (e.g., overexposure, chemical burn)

4. Recognize the values of the pH scale

DOMAIN 2: HAIR CARE AND SERVICES (45%)

2A Hair Care and Services - Client Consultation, Analysis, and Documentation

1. Evaluate condition of client's hair and scalp

2. Recognize conditions that would prohibit service (i.e., contraindications)

3. Utilize preliminary tests (e.g., predisposition and strand tests)

4. Recommend services or products based on client needs

5. Establish/Maintain client records (e.g., service history, client card, medical history)

2B Hair Care and Services - Tools used in Hair Care Services

1. Identify purpose, function, and infection control procedures of items

    a. Equipment (e.g., chair, workstation)

    b. Implements (e.g., razors, shears, combs/brushes)

    c. Supplies and materials (e.g., towels, drapes, neck strips)

    d. Electrical tools (e.g. irons, blow dryers, clippers)

2. Demonstrate safe practices

    a. Tools/Implements

    b. Ergonomics

2C Hair Care and Services - Hair Care Principles and Procedures

1. Demonstrate shampooing and conditioning

2. Demonstrate scalp treatments and scalp massage

3. Demonstrate draping (e.g. chemical, shampoo, cutting, styling)

4. Recognize differences in Hair Care principles and procedures based on various hair types and textures

2D Hair Care and Services - Hair Design Principles and Procedures

1. Demonstrate hair cutting and shaping

2. Demonstrate hair styling:

    a. Wet styling

    b. Thermal styling

    c. Natural hair styling (e.g., braiding)

3. Apply, maintain, and remove hair enhancements:

    a. Wigs and hairpieces

    b. Hair additions (i.e., taping, bonding, fusion, linking)

4. Apply principles of balance and design (e.g. facial shape, physical structure)

5. Recognize differences in Hair Design principles and procedures based on various hair types and textures

2E Hair Care and Services - Chemical Services Principles, and Procedures

1. Perform hair color services (e.g., virgin, retouch, lightening, foiling, balayage, color formulation, color correction)

2. Perform chemical hair relaxer/restructurizer and curl reduction (e.g., hydroxide, thio, keratin) service

3. Perform chemical waving/texturizing (e.g., alkaline, acid, non-thio) services

4. Understand the chemical products used for the various hair texture types

DOMAIN 3: SKIN CARE AND SERVICES (10%)

3A Skin Care and Services - Client Consultation, Analysis, and Documentation

    1. Evaluate the client's skin:

        a. Skin type

        b. Skin condition

    2. Recognize conditions that would prohibit service (i.e., contraindications)

    3. Recommend services or products based on client needs

    4. Establish/Maintain client records (e.g., service history, client card, medical history)

3B Skin Care and Services - Tools used for Skin Care Services

    1. Identify purpose, function, and infection control procedures of items:

        a. Equipment (e.g., chair, steamer)

        b. Implements (e.g., tweezers, brushes, extractors)

        c. Supplies, products, and materials (e.g., creams, masks, towels, wax, head coverings)

    2. Demonstrate safe practices

        a. Tools/implements

        b. Ergonomics

3C Skin Care and Services - Skin Care Principles and Procedures

    1. Apply knowledge of a basic facial

    2. Apply knowledge of hair removal

    3. Apply knowledge of makeup application

    4. Apply knowledge of electrical equipment

DOMAIN 4: NAIL CARE AND SERVICES (10%)

4A Nail Care and Services - Client Consultation, Analysis, and Documentation

1. Evaluate condition of client's nails
2. Recognize conditions that would prohibit service (i.e., contraindications)
3. Recommend services or products based on client needs
4. Establish/Maintain client records (e.g., service history, client card, medical history)

4B Nail Care and Services - Tools used in Nail Care Services

1. Identify purpose, function, and infection control procedures of items:
   a. Equipment (e.g., workstation, pedicure basin)
   b. Implements (e.g., nippers, file)
   c. Supplies, products, and materials (e.g., towels, creams, polish)
2. Demonstrate safe practices
   a. Tools/implements
   b. Ergonomics

4C Nail Care and Services - Nail Service Principles and Procedures

1. Apply knowledge of a basic manicure and pedicure
2. Apply, maintain, and remove nail enhancements

Practical Exam

The scope of the National Cosmetology Practical Examination includes 10 core domain sections. The Core Domain Sections are based on the national job analysis.

1. Work Area and Client Preparation, and Set Up of Supplies (First client 15 minutes)
2. Thermal Curling (10 minutes)
3. Haircutting (30 minutes)
4. Work Area and New Client Preparation, and Set Up of Supplies (Second client 15 minutes)
5. Chemical Waving (20 minutes)
6. Predisposition Test and Strand Test with Simulated Product (10 minutes)
7. Highlighting with Foil, Virgin Application with Colored Simulated Product (15 minutes)
8. Hair Color Retouch with Colored Simulated Product (10 minutes)
9. Virgin Hair Relaxer Application with Colored Simulated Product (Untimed)
10. Blood Exposure Procedure (10 minutes)

California Additional Services
14. Basic Facial (20 minutes) (Performed on Client 2)
20. Sculptured Nail (20 minutes) (Performed on Client 2)

It is recommended that you pack your supplies in sealable plastic bags, grouped and labeled for each respective procedure.

The list of supplies with an (*) next to them means they aren't required by all states, so it is best you check with your state to see if they are required.

Thermal Curling Supplies
- Marcel iron
- Heat-resistant Comb
- Material for testing temperature of iron

Hair Cutting Supplies
- Hair Cutting shears
- Razor
- Comb(s)
- Chemical Waving Supplies

Chemical wave rods
- End papers
- Applicator bottle with simulated waving lotion (water)
- Comb(s)

Hair Lightening/Coloring Supplies
- Tint brush and bowl or bottle applicator
- Thick gel or colored cholesterol*
- Comb(s)
- Hair clips

Chemical Relaxing Supplies
- Tint brush and bowl or bottle applicator
- Thick gel or colored cholesterol*
- Comb(s) *

Blow Dry Styling Supplies
- Blow dryer
- Hairbrush(es)

Shaping & Pin Curl Shaping Supplies
- Clippies

- Gel
- Comb(s) *

Roller Placement Supplies
- Clippies
- Rollers
- Comb(s)

Basic Facial Supplies
- Hair drape
- Cleansing cream
- Massage cream
- Toner or astringent

Manicure Supplies
- Mannequin hand(s) with artificial nails attached* (Trainer hands are NOT permitted.)
- Bowl and container of water
- Cuticle cream/remover
- Filing and buffing implements
- Cuticle pusher
- Nail brush
- Hand lotion or massage product
- Cuticle oil
- Base coat
- Top coat
- Red polish
- Polish remover *

Sculptured Nail Supplies
- Mannequin hand(s) with artificial nails attached* (Trainer hands are NOT permitted.)
- Cuticle pusher

- Sculptured nail products (powder, primer, liquid) (The product must be sealed and in its original container with the manufacturer's label. NIC strongly recommends, due to the testing environment, that odorless sculptured nail products be used during the NIC practical examinations.)
- Sculptured nail brush
- Liquid & powder containers
- Filing and buffing implements
- Sculptured nail forms

Hair Removal of The Eyebrows Supplies
- Antiseptic
- Tweezers
- Gloves
- Fabric strips
- Soft wax product/simulated product*
- Post epilation product
- Applicators

Recommended General Supplies
- Dry storage kit/container*
- Hand sanitizer
- Mannequin head(s) and a table clamp* (pre-marked mannequins are NOT permitted)
- A towel to place between the clamp and the table*
- EPA registered disinfectant that demonstrates bactericidal, fungicidal and virucidal properties must be used*
- Container/bag for soiled/trash items ¨ container or bag for items to be disinfected*
- Cloth and paper towel(s)
- Neck strip(s)
- Shampoo cape (child size is appropriate for mannequin)
- Hair clamp(s)

- Comb(s)
- Hair brush(es)
- Spray bottle
- Protective cream
- Spatula(s)
- Protective cotton
- Protective gloves
- First aid supplies (blood spill kit)
- Tape

Don't forget to bring your pen to sign into the examination.

Eligibility Requirements for the Cosmetology State Board Exam

To become a cosmetologist, you must be at least sixteen to eighteen years old, depending on your state laws. Some states also require you have a high school diploma or GED, while others require schooling up to a certain grade level.

Every state has a designated number of educational hours required before you can take a test to obtain your cosmetology license. This number varies, but you can generally complete your hours in less than a year if you are dedicated and take many classes. However, some states require a timeframe of up to two years of experience, along with your educational hours.

After obtaining your license, you will also need to continue your education with additional hours every so often. This is required in order to renew your license and continue legally working as a cosmetologist.

Common questions about the cosmetology license:

Q: Can I get a cosmetology license without going to school?

A: Every state requires that you attend an accredited school to get your cosmetology license.

If you don't want to (or can't) be in class every day, there are now plenty of online cosmetology schools available – which you can "attend" instead of a physical school.

But be aware that you'll still need to have a specific number of hands-on training hours to qualify – which means you'll be expected to attend in person for the practical portions of the program. (Alternatively, you might be able to find a local salon that will allow you to intern there in order to acquire your necessary training hours. It depends what your state allows.)

Q: Can I use my cosmetology license in any state?

A: If you're moving to a new state, you'll usually be able to transfer your license – but you MUST transfer your license before you can work there legally.

Many states have reciprocity agreements with each other, in which one state allows you to work under the license of your home state.

Other states will license you by endorsement. To qualify, your new state must agree that your home state has similar training requirements and board exams. If you meet their criteria, the new state will endorse your license – which will allow you to work legally there.

Both these methods usually allow you to avoid taking any more examinations – and the method you use will depend on the state you're moving to.

To get started, call the new state's licensing board to ask whether you qualify for reciprocity/endorsement and what the conditions are. (Some states will require that you've worked for a minimum numbers of years to qualify.) There may be a service fee to transfer your license.

How to Apply for the Cosmetology State Board Exam

Before you register for your exam, we recommend you understand what your study needs are. If you haven't started studying for the exam yet, don't register to take the test two weeks from now.

Review the exam study sheet and assess how comfortable you are with the material you will be getting tested on. For best practice, we recommend 3-5 months of studying before taking the exam (1-2 months if you're using Cosmetology Guru).

If you want to register to take the exam you can do it over the phone: Call PSI at (800) 733-9267 Monday through Friday between 7:30 am and 10:00 pm, and Saturday-Sunday between 9:00 am and 5:30 pm, Eastern Time.

Over the Internet: Visit PSI Exams, click 'Register' for examination. PSI will make every effort to schedule the examination site and time that is most convenient for you. You may schedule an examination 1 day prior to the examination date of your choice, up to 7:00 p.m.

32

State Board Exam Day Requirements

As your exam day begins to approach, it is important to be aware of the requirements you have to meet in order to be able to take your exam.

On the day you come to take your Cosmetology State Board Exam, you must have finished your training program and all of your hours must be reported by your school or referring program.

You are required to provide originals of qualifying pieces of identification. Your name on your identification is required to match your name exactly as listed in your online account.

Two forms of government issued identification are required. One piece of identification must include a current photo. Your name is required to match on both forms unless you also bring documentation of name change (for example, official court document indicating name change).

Accepted as Identification Original Identification With Photo:
- U.S. or foreign driver's license – valid, or expired within one year
- U.S. armed services ID card – with photo and signature
- U.S. or foreign passport – valid, or expired within one year
- Federal or state employee ID Card – valid, shows your signature and photo
- State issued ID card with photo – valid, or expired within one year

- Immigration ID – valid, with signature from the U.S. Citizenship and Immigration Service
- U.S. Certificate of Citizenship or Naturalization – with signature and photo
- U.S. Permanent Resident Card – valid, with your signature and photo
- Tribal ID card
- U.S. Veteran's Administration ID card – valid with photo Original Identification Without Photo
- Certified birth certificate – original or certified document
- Social Security card (not laminated) or Tax Payer ID letter
- U.S. government-issued work visa – valid
- Voter's card
- Medicare card
- Social Security Administration receipt of name change / replacement card

If you are unable to meet the identification requirements noted above, please contact National Testing Network (NTN) at 1-866-563-3882.

You are required to provide biometric authentication and your digital signature when you check in on exam day.

Prohibited Items and Behavior in the Exam Room

Prohibited Items:

- Reference materials of any kind.
- Electronic devices of any type.
- Hats or headgear not worn for religious reasons or as religious apparel, including hats, baseball caps, or visors.
- Bulky or loose clothing or coats including but not limited to, open sweaters, cardigans, shawls, scarves, vests, jackets, and coats.
- Other personal items, including but not limited to; backpacks, briefcases, chewing gum, drinks, food, good luck items, notebooks, paper or other materials on which to write, pens, pencils or other writing devices, purses, reading material, smoking or chewing products, wallets, etc.

No prohibited items are allowed within the candidate's reach or line of sight. If prohibited items are found during check-in, candidates shall put them in the provided secure storage or return these items to their vehicle for test center exams.

Prohibited Behavior:

- Giving or receiving assistance on an examination.
- Copying or communicating examination content.
- Using outside references or resources during an exam. Some examples:
- Browsing the internet.

- Using notepad on the computer.
- Using an application on the computer not provided by PSI.
- Reading questions out loud.
- Leaving the room without proctor approval.
- Using instant messaging, or other electronic communication.
- Capturing a picture or video of exam items.
- Attempting to use telephone or mobile device.
- Obstructing the proctor's view (camera or in person).
- Having inappropriate materials on desktop (explicit).
- Changing spaces during the exam without proctor approval.
- Not focusing eyes on the screen.

During the check in process, all candidates will be asked if they possess any prohibited items. They will be asked to raise their pant legs to ensure that notes or recording devices are not being hidden there.

Additional protocols for testing at a testing center, include but not limited to:

- Person(s) accompanying an examination candidate may not wait in the examination center, inside the building, or on the building's property. This applies to guests of any nature, including drivers, children, friends, family, colleagues, or instructors.
- Once candidates have been seated and the examination begins, they may leave the examination room only to use the restroom, and only after obtaining permission from the proctor. Candidates will not receive extra time to complete the examination.

Additional protocols for taking your examination on your laptop or computer, include but not limited to:

- Temporarily moving out of the camera's line of sight.
- Adequate lighting for the proctor to see candidate's activity.
- Web camera must be placed for ideal viewing by the proctor.
- Candidate may not change computers during the exam.
- Candidate may not change spaces during the exam.
- Please do your best to avoid covering your mouth for the whole duration of exam.
- Breaks are NOT allowed during remote online proctored examinations.
- Candidate must follow proctor instructions, which may include, but are not limited to:
  - Keeping hands on the desktop.
  - Keeping eyes on the computer screen.
  - Keeping hands away from face.

Common questions about the exam

Q: What's the passing score for the cosmetology written exam?

A: There's no universal passing score: each state chooses its own pass rate. In California, for example, cosmetologists, estheticians, manicurists, and barbers all need to score at least 75% to pass both the written and practical exams.

Q: How many questions are on the cosmetology state board written exam?

A: The written examination in all states is a computer-based, multiple-choice examination. There are usually 100 questions – but the precise number of questions varies from state to state.

The written examinations may contain 10 additional questions, which are placed randomly throughout the examination. These questions are being assessed for inclusion on future versions of the exam, and they won't count towards or against your score.

The specific questions will vary from day to day: no set of questions will be identical to previous days.

Q: How long does the state board cosmetology test take?

A: The time allocated for the cosmetology written test varies from state to state, so you'll need to check with your local state board. Here's some information for some of the most popular cosmetology states:

- The California State Board of Cosmetology has 100 written questions for cosmetologists, estheticians and manicurists (and 120 minutes in which to complete them). For barbers, there are 50 questions and 90 minutes.
- The Alabama Board of Cosmetology has 100 written questions for cosmetologists, barbers, estheticians and manicurists (and 90 minutes to complete them).
- The Louisiana Board of Cosmetology has 100 written questions for cosmetologists, barbers, estheticians and manicurists (and 90 minutes to complete them).

Q: Is the cosmetology state board written test multiple choice?

A: Yes: in all states, the written examination is a computer-based, multiple-choice examination. There are usually 100 questions – but the precise number of questions varies from state to state.

Q: When do I find out my results?

A: You will get the written results via email within seven working days.

Exam Preparation Tips

How to Structure Your Study Sessions

This book contains the KEY facts you need to know and nothing else – ensuring you don't waste any time on unnecessary information. There's no filler, no fluff, and no unnecessary details – allowing you to learn and memorize everything much more quickly than any other book or study guide out there.

But, you'll be setting yourself up for failure if your study strategy involves simply skimming this book the night before the exam. Yes: it contains all the need-to-know information, but you need to know that information! And you need to understand it, too – to enable you to answer questions that are asked in an unfamiliar way, or questions that are structured in a way that's different from what you're used to.

Daunted? Don't be. In this chapter you'll learn how to structure your study sessions to ensure you're prepared and ready to pass on exam day. Let's get started...

1. Start with the official written exam breakdown of the domains

Start by paying attention to the weighting of each domain. For example, "Hair Care and Services" takes up 45% of the exam's content – so be sure to devote a particularly large chunk of time to reminding yourself of the key aspects of the domain.

Next, look at the topics within each domain. How well do you know and understand each of them? You could write a percentage amount next to each topic, representing how well you think you know it.

Then, when you go through the rest of the book, devote time to really digging into those topics you're less familiar with. You can update each "topic percentage" as you improve your understanding of it – a nice, visual way of marking your progress.

2. Discover which study method suits you best – and use it

According to experts, different people have different learning styles – meaning some people retain information more easily when it is presented via one format or method, while others prefer a totally different style. While there's some disagreement on precisely how many learning styles there are (anywhere up to seven!), we've found that four learning styles in particular seem to cover most students. These are:

- Visual learning

- Reading/writing learning

- Auditory (listening) learning

- Kinesthetic (physical participation) learning

Visual learners enjoy using pictures, images, and graphics for learning. In order to absorb information and "make it stick," visual learners like to rely on drawing, doodling, color-coding, and making posters. They tend to process information better when it is presented as a whole rather than piecemeal – so it's a good idea to use charts and diagrams that summarize information rather than sequential slides of information.

Reading/writing learners enjoy the written word. Whether it's PowerPoint slides, textbooks, or text-heavy websites, they can synthesize the information well. They also tend to absorb information and recall it easily later by writing things down – so they do well when taking copious notes during lectures, for example.

Auditory learners often struggle to read things silently, and may move their lips or talk quietly when writing something down. They learn better through songs, audiobooks, podcasts, stories, and discussion. Another great way for auditory learners to learn is by absorbing the information (e.g. by listening to it or reading it out loud to themselves), then teaching that information to someone else.

Kinesthetic learners benefit from using their bodies to learn. They need to be involved in making projects, role playing, and learning while standing or moving around. If you struggle to sit still and find yourself pacing while trying to absorb new information, there's a good chance you're a kinesthetic learner!

It's unlikely you'll fit neatly into one specific type of learning: you might find you like to combine listening to information then writing it down, for example. Even so, knowing these learning styles and identifying which appeal to you will help you structure your study time better. If you know you're at least partially an auditory learner, you could read out sections of this book and record them, then listen to the recordings later. Or if you know you enjoy learning visually, you can create charts and diagrams out of some of the information.

3. Make sure you're retaining the information

Whichever learning style you prefer, you will need to assess if it's effective – that is, you must make sure that you're actually retaining the information. So how can you check?

Flashcards are a useful first step. You can create your own, or there are plenty to buy online (make sure they reflect the most recent changes to the exam). Take them everywhere you go, and use any spare moment to review them. If you start to find particular flashcards "easy" (i.e. you know them and understand them right away), remove them from the pack so you have more time to focus on the topics you find trickier.

Next up: practice tests. **This book has an accompanying online study package called Cosmetology Guru Online (www.cosmetologyguru.com),** which contains hundreds of realistic practice questions. With our practice questions, you can focus on one domain at a time, or mix them all up.

After you've worked your way through the practice questions and you feel confident about your knowledge, it's time to test your expertise with a simulated exam! **Cosmetology Guru Online** contains six simulated exams, which replicate the real-life exam you'll be taking. They contain a true representation of the types of questions you'll be asked in the real thing, and they'll be timed – allowing you to get used to the full exam experience.

Buy Cosmetology Guru Online and get:

- Hundreds of practice questions
- Six simulated exams
- A condensed version of this book – so you can learn on your device whenever you have a spare moment

Visit www.cosmetologyguru.com and enter 30OFFNOW at checkout for 30% off.

Tips for How to Approach the Exam

Here are some of our tried-and-true methods:

1. Pay attention to every instruction – the testing environment minimizes distractions, but you may get nervous or anxious and skim important details in your rush. So, pay close attention to your exam.
2. Read the entire test – concentrate on each question in the written exam. Breathe deeply and avoid becoming overwhelmed. Take it slowly. You can always come back to answer any difficult questions later if you're unsure about them or don't know the answer.
3. Eliminate all incorrect answers until you're left with the right one.
4. If you're stuck at one question, move on and get back to it at the end.
5. Pace yourself - It's easy to feel daunted and overwhelmed when you first start the exam: 100 questions all needing to be read, contemplated, and answered. But don't rush: you have plenty of time. If you find you have less time than you think toward the end of the exam, stay calm: it's far better that you use those minutes to answer a few questions correctly than to rush through and answer everything incorrectly.
6. Check your work - Once you've answered all the questions, there should be enough time to go back through the entire exam and double check your answer selections. Even though you've read each question carefully, eliminated incorrect

answers, and made use of all the other tips on this list, there's still a chance you made a careless mistake.

You can increase your chances of success and reduce stress by mentally and physically preparing for one of your career's most important (maybe even life-changing) moments. So, take your time, study diligently, and best of luck!

Scientific Concepts

Infection Control: Federal Agencies

Environmental Protection Agency (EPA)

The EPA is responsible for licensing disinfecting agents. Every label on a disinfectant must have an EPA registration number.

Disinfectants used in salons will be classified as either "hospital grade" or "tuberculocidal":

- **Hospital grade disinfectants** can clean and disinfect blood and bodily fluids in hospitals.

- **Tuberculocidal disinfectants** kill bacteria – specifically those that cause tuberculosis. Tuberculocidals can be too strong for salon tools (and may cause damage), so it's important to know which grade of disinfectant you're using.

Occupational Safety and Health Administration (OSHA)

OSHA was created to regulate and enforce health and safety standards in the workplace.

Among other things, it requires that chemical manufacturers supply purchasers with a **Safety Data Sheet (SDS)** – formerly known as a **Material Safety Data Sheet (MSDS)** – for all potentially harmful products sold. The SDS contains information about hazardous ingredients in the product, safe handling and use instructions, and precautions to reduce the risk of fire, burns, overexposure, etc.

Federal law requires that every school, beauty school, barber shop, and nail salon must have an SDS available on the premises for each product – which must be available during regular business hours. (If not, fines can be issued.)

OSHA publishes guidelines called **Universal Precautions**, which require the employer and employee to assume that all human blood and body fluids are infectious for bloodborne pathogens.

Infections

Infectious organisms ("germs") can cause infectious diseases if they're not eliminated or controlled. For cosmetologists, the four most important types of infectious organisms are **bacteria, viruses, fungi** and **parasites**:

Bacteria

Bacteria (AKA germs or microbes) are one-celled microorganisms.

Some are harmful (**pathogenic bacteria**) and cause disease and infections when they invade plant or animal tissue. Other forms of bacteria are helpful (**non-pathogenic bacteria**).

Most bacteria come in one of the following basic shapes:

- **Cocci** are round-shaped bacteria that appear alone or in groups and can cause **boils, strep throat, pneumonia**, and other diseases.

- **Bacilli** are rod-shaped and are the most common bacteria. They produce diseases including **tetanus, septicemia, meningitis**, and **urinary tract infections**.

- **Spirilla** are spiral or corkscrew-shaped bacteria that cause **syphilis** and **Lyme disease**, among others.
  Bacilli and spirilla move about by using long, thin, hair-like structures called **flagella** (AKA **cilia**).

Bacterial spores are highly resistant structures that help organisms survive during adverse environmental conditions (such as famine, dryness, and unsuitable temperatures). They are not harmed by disinfectants, heat or cold.

Mitosis is the reproduction process of bacteria during its active stage. During this stage, bacteria replicate then divide into identical new cells called daughter cells.

Viruses

Viruses are small infectious agents that are submicroscopic in size. They infect and live inside the cells of other living organisms. Common viruses include the **common cold**, **ear infections**, and **gastroenteritis**.

- **HIV** is a type of virus. It's spread through blood and bodily fluids. A person can be infected for many years without having symptoms.

  If you accidentally cut a client, the tool will be contaminated with whatever might be in the person's blood – including HIV. You must clean and disinfect the implement before reusing.

- **Hepatitis** is a blood borne virus that causes the disease and can damage the liver. It can live on surfaces outside the body for long periods of time, so it's vital that all surfaces that contact a client are thoroughly cleaned and disinfected. Hepatitis B is the most difficult to kill on a surface, so check the label of the disinfectant to make sure it's effective against Hepatitis B.

Infection control in the facial area is necessary to help prevent the spread of Hepatitis.

- **Fungi** are microscopic **plant parasites** (different from regular parasites – see below) that cause disease and sometimes death of the host. Fungi include mold, mildews, and yeast. They can also produce contagious diseases such as **ringworm**.

You may come across many types of fungal infection in a salon. The most common are:

- o **Folliculitis barbae** (AKA **barbers itch** or **hot tub folliculitis**), which is an inflammation of hair follicles.
- o **Tinea barbae** is primarily limited to the bearded areas of the face and neck or around the scalp. It causes deep, inflamed or non-inflamed patches of skin.
- o **Tinea capitis** is a fungal infection of the scalp. It causes red papules (spots) at the opening of the hair follicles. More on this later.
- o **Tinea pedis** is a ringworm fungus of the foot.

Remember: fungi are plant parasites, which are different from "regular"/animal parasites mentioned below.

- **Parasites** are animals/organisms that grow, feed, and take shelter on other living matter ("the host"), while contributing nothing to the survival of the host. Examples of parasites include **head lice** and **scabies**. There's more information on head lice and scabies in the section on Hair Care and Services.

Immunity

Immunity is the ability of the body to destroy any bacteria that have entered, and to resist infection in general. Immunity can be **natural** (partly inherited, and partly developed through healthy living) or **acquired** (develops after the body overcomes a disease, or through inoculation.

Preventing infection

Decontamination

Decontamination refers to a combination of processes that remove or destroy infectious agents/other contaminants so that they cannot cause infection or other forms of harm. There are three steps involved in decontamination, but only the first two are used in salons:

1. **Cleaning (AKA sanitation) is the only type of infection control process that can be used on humans or other living things.** It involves removing all visible dirt and debris from tools, implements, and equipment by washing with liquid soap and warm water. You must also use a nail brush to scrub grooved or hinged portions of the item.

   The proper protocol for hand washing is as follows:

   Using a paper towel, turn on the warm water and lather and scrub hands with liquid antibacterial soap for 15 seconds.

   While soap, water, and a brush are the only products that can clean the skin, **waterless hand sanitizers (AKA antiseptics)** can reduce the number or slow down the growth of microbes on the skin. **They're the only type of chemical germicides that can be used on the skin, and they're regulated by the FDA.**

   The vast majority of contaminants and pathogens can be removed through proper cleaning, which reduces the risk of spreading infection. It doesn't mean the object/surface is free from disease-causing germs – just that those germs have been reduced to a safe level.

2. **Disinfection** with an appropriate EPA-registered disinfectant is the second step in infection control (in salons): **it eliminates most microorganisms (bacteria, fungi, and viruses) and other pathogens on non-porous surfaces such as cuticle nippers and scissors**. Note that the process is *not* effective on bacterial spores.

   Never use disinfectants to clean skin, hair, or nails.

   Disinfectants must have efficacy claims on the label – which refers to the effectiveness with which the product kills microorganisms.

The third and final step is **sterilization**. This is the only process that destroys ALL microbial life (including spores). This level of decontamination is required in medical settings and any place where intentional puncturing of the skin occurs, but rarely in salons.

Effective sterilization normally requires the use of an **autoclave** – equipment that incorporates heat and pressure.

Contagious infections/diseases

When a disease spreads from one person to another, it's known as a **contagious** (AKA **communicable**) disease. Some of the most common contagious diseases are:

- The common cold
- Ringworm
- Conjunctivitis (pinkeye)

- Viral infections
- Natural nail, toe, or foot infections

You cannot perform a service on a client who has a contagious disease.

General important safety and prevention rules

- Any items used to perform a salon service on a client must be disinfected or discarded (depending on whether they're single-use/disposable or multiuse/reusable items).
- Implements must be thoroughly cleaned before they are immersed in disinfectant.
- Never remove implements from disinfectants with bare fingers.
- Liquid disinfectants must be prepared fresh every day.
- When mixing disinfectants, it's important to add disinfectant to water – not the other way around. If you add water to the disinfectant, the resulting mixture will be a foam. It's hard to measure the ratios of foam, and you may end up with a mixture that's either too diluted or not diluted enough.
- Once implements have been disinfected, they should be stored in a disinfected and covered container.
- If any multiuse implements become contaminated with blood during the service, they must be placed in your container for "dirty" items. Surfaces must be sprayed or wiped with an approved disinfectant.
- If any single-use objects such as wipes or cotton balls become contaminated with blood, they must be placed in a plastic bag. The plastic bag must then be placed in a closed trash container with a liner bag. Sharp disposables must be deposited in a sharps box and then disposed of according to state/local law.
- If you cut yourself or your client during a service…

- First, stop the service and tell your client what has happened and that you're taking care of the cut.
- Put on gloves (or – if receiving assistance – have the salon employee put on gloves). When appropriate, wash the injury with soap and water. Apply slight pressure to the wound with cotton to stop the bleeding, then cleanse the area with an antiseptic. Note: pressure stops the bleeding – NOT the antiseptic.

- Soiled towels and linens must be stored separately from clean towels and linens – and must not be used again until they have been properly laundered.
- During a chemical service, soiled towels must be replaced immediately with clean ones (on the client).

General rules for cleaning and disinfecting

Note: **ALL disinfectants used in salons must be "broad spectrum"**. That is, they must be bactericidal (capable of destroying bacteria), virucidal (capable of destroying viruses), AND fungicidal (capable of destroying fungi).

- Nonelectrical tools and implements (combs, brushes, clips, metal bushes, tweezers, etc.) must be immersed in a disinfection container holding an EPA-registered disinfectant for the required time (at least 10 minutes or according to the manufacturer's instructions).

- Whirlpool, air-jet, and pipeless foot spas require that EPA-registered hospital disinfectant is circulated through the basin before and after chelating detergent is used. (Chelating detergent is a cleanser designed for use in hard water, and is not required in all states.)

- **Basic foot basins and tubs** must be filled with EPA-registered hospital disinfectant for 10 minutes (or according to the manufacturer's instructions).

Anatomy & physiology

Cells, tissues and organs

Cells are organized into layers/groups called **tissues**. Groups of tissues form complex structures called **organs**, which perform certain functions.

Here's some more detail:

- **Cells** are the basic building blocks of all living things (including human bodies). They provide structure for the body and also carry out certain specialized functions depending on the type of cell.

  The nucleus of the cell contains most of the DNA (which is each person's unique genetic code). It is also serves as the control center for cell metabolism, growth, and reproduction.

- **Tissues** are groupings of cells in specific structures to perform specific functions. These tissues then make up organs and various parts of the body. There are four main types of tissue:

  - **Muscle tissue** contracts and moves various parts of the body.
  - **Epithelial tissue** is the fat that provides a protective covering on body surfaces (such as skin, mucous membranes, the lining of the heart, and the glands).
  - **Connective tissue** holds our body parts together. Examples include bone, cartilage, ligaments,

tendons, blood, lymph, and adipose tissue (a technical term for fat).
- o **Nerve tissue** controls and coordinates all bodily functions by carrying messages to and from the brain. It is made up of special cells called neurons.

- **Organs** are the body's recognizable structures that perform specific functions. Each organ is composed of many types of tissue (and therefore many types of cells). Some examples of organs are:

  - o The **heart** is the organ that circulates the body's blood.
  - o The **lungs** supply oxygen to the blood.
  - o The **skin** covers the body and is the external protective coating. The skin is the largest organ of the human body.

Body systems

There are 11 body systems in total:

1. The **circulatory system** controls the movement of blood throughout the body.
2. The **digestive (gastrointestinal) system** breaks food down into nutrients or waste for nutrition or excretion.
3. The **endocrine system** controls hormone levels within the body. These levels determine growth, development, sexual function, and general bodily health.
4. The **excretory system** eliminates waste from the body, thus reducing the buildup of toxins. One example is the skin, which excretes waste through perspiration ("sweating").

5. The **integumentary system** provides protective covering and regulates the body temperature.
6. The **immune (lymphatic) system** protects the body from disease by developing immunities and destroying toxins and pathogens.
7. The **muscular system** covers, shapes, and holds the skeleton in place. Muscles contract to allow for body structures to move.
8. The **nervous system** coordinates all other body systems, allowing them to work efficiently and react to their environment.
9. The **reproductive system** produces offspring and allows for the transfer of genetic material.
10. The **respiratory system** makes blood and oxygen available to body structures through respiration. It eliminates carbon dioxide.
11. The **skeletal system** forms the physical foundation of the body: 206 bones that are connected by movable and immovable joints.

Skin structure, growth, and nutrition

Anatomy of the skin

The skin is composed of two main divisions: the epidermis and the dermis.

- The **epidermis** is the outermost and thinnest layer of the skin, which protects the body from the environment. It doesn't contain any blood vessels, but it has many small nerve endings. It is made up of five layers:

- The **stratum corneum** (AKA **horny layer**) is the outermost layer: it's the layer we see when we look at the skin, and the layer cared for by salon products and services. As the horny layer is the outermost layer of the epidermis, it is the one that protects the body from the environment.

- The **stratum lucidum** is a clear, transparent layer under the stratum corneum.

- The **stratum granulosum** (AKA **granular layer**) is composed of cells that looks like granules and are filled with keratin. Keratin is a fibrous protein of cells. It is also the principal component of hair and nails.

- The **stratum spinosum** is the spiny layer where the process of skin cell shedding begins.

- The **stratum germinativum** (AKA **basal cell layer**) is the deepest layer of the epidermis. It produces new epidermal skin cells and is responsible for the growth of the epidermis. It also contains cells called **melanocytes**, which produce the dark skin pigment called **melanin** (discussed later).

- The **dermis** (AKA **derma, corium, cutis,** or **true skin**) is the underlying/inner layer of the skin, **extending to form the subcutaneous tissue.**

The dermis contains many **blood vessels, sebaceous (oil) glands, sudoriferous (sweat) glands, lymph vessels,** nerves, **hair follicles,** and **arrector pili muscles** (the small, involuntary muscles in the base of the hair follicle that cause "goose flesh" (AKA **goose bumps**) and papillae.

The outer layer of the dermis (the papillary layer) also contains some more melanocytes – the pigment-producing cells.

Skin color

The color of the skin (whether fair, medium, or dark) depends mostly on **melanin.** Melanin is tiny grains of pigment (coloring matter) that are deposited into cells in the basal layer of the epidermis and the papillary layer of the dermis.
The body produces two types of melanin:

- **Eumelanin** is a dark brown to black pigment. People with dark-colored skin mostly produce eumelanin.
- **Pheomelanin** is a red and/or yellow pigment. People with light-colored skin mostly produce pheomelanin.

Melanin helps prevent sensitive cells from the sun's UV light, but it doesn't provide enough protection to prevent skin damage. To help the melanin protect the skin from burning, skin cancer, and premature aging, it's important to apply a broad spectrum (protecting against both UV-A and UV-B radiation) sunscreen daily.

Strength and flexibility of the skin

The skin gets its strength, flexibility, and form from two structures in the dermis: collagen and elastin. Both are made of flexible protein fibers, and they make up 70% of the dermis.

- **Collagen** gives the skin form and strength. When collagen fibers are healthy, the skin is able to stretch and contract as needed.

- **Elastin** forms elastic tissue. It is interwoven with collagen, and gives the skin its flexibility and elasticity – helping the skin retain its shape, even after being repeatedly stretched or expanded.

When these protein fibers become weakened due to age, lack of moisture, frequent changes in weight, and – particularly – **sun exposure** (according to a majority of scientists), the skin will become less toned and supple, leading to wrinkles and sagging.

Glands of the skin

The skin (specifically the dermis) contains two kinds of duct glands that extract materials from the blood to form new substances:

- **Sebaceous (oil) glands** sit in the skin and are connected to the hair follicles. They secrete a fatty/oily substance called sebum, which lubricates the skin and maintains the softness of the hair. (**Sebaceous glands are glands of excretion**.)

  These glands are found everywhere except the palms of the hands and the soles of the feet. They're particularly numerous in the face and scalp, where they're larger. There's more on sebaceous glands in the sections on skin care and hair care.

- **Sudoriferous (sweat) glands** detoxify the body by excreting excess salt and unwanted chemicals through perspiration. As well as eliminating waste products from the body, these glands also regulate body temperature:

when sweat evaporates, it cools the skin's surface. (In your exam, you may be asked which organ regulates body temperature. The answer would be the skin. If you're asked which body system regulates body temperature, the answer would be the integumentary system.)

These glands are found in most parts of the body, but are most numerous on the palms of the hands, the soles of the feet, forehead, and underarms (armpits).

The excretion of perspiration and flow of sebum are controlled/regulated by **secretory nerves**, which are part of the automatic nervous system.

Disorders of the skin

Disorders of the sebaceous (oil) glands

- **Open comedones** (AKA **blackheads**) are hair follicles impacted with solidified sebum and dead keratin buildup. When the sebum is exposed to the environment, it oxidizes and turns black.

  They're most frequently found on people with oily skin, which produces too much sebum. The skin will have large pores.

  (Remember: sebum is a fatty/oily secretion that lubricates the skin and maintains the softness of the hair. Keratin is a fibrous protein that's the key structural component of hair and nails.)

- **Closed comedones** (AKA **whiteheads**) are also frequently found on people with oily skin. When the impacted hair follicles are closed and not exposed to the environment, the sebum remains a white/cream color, and it appears as small bumps under the skin's surface.

- **Milia** are benign, keratin-filled cysts that appear just under the epidermis, and resemble small sesame seeds. While commonly found on newborn babies, they're often found on the eyes, cheeks, and forehead of people of all ages. They are firm in texture, whereas whiteheads are softer.

- **Acne** (AKA **acne vulgaris**) is found in oily areas of skin, where there is an abundance of sebum in each follicle. Bacteria flourish and multiply in this oily environment, causing inflammation and swelling in the follicle. Eventually, the follicle wall ruptures – which in turn alerts the immune system and causes blood to rush to the follicle, carrying white blood cells to fight the bacteria. Blood surrounds the follicle, which is what causes the redness in acne pimples.

  Acne pimples (called **papules**) do not have a pus head. Pimples with a pus head are called **pustules**. Pus is fluid inside a pustule, made up of dead white blood cells that tried to fight the infection.

  Papules and pustules are larger than blackheads and whiteheads.

- **Sebaceous cysts** are large, protruding lesions filled with sebum. They're most often seen on the scalp and back, and can be surgically removed by a dermatologist.

- **Seborrheic dermatitis** is caused by an inflammation of the sebaceous glands. It often appears in the eyebrows and beard, in the scalp and hairline, at the middle of the forehead, and along the sides of the nose. It consists of an accumulation of waxy or greasy scales, mixed with sebum, that stick to the skin in crusts. The skin has a red, flaky, crusty, and dry/oily scaling appearance, often accompanied by itching.

   Almost all cases should be seen by a dermatologist, who'll often prescribe topical antifungal medications.

- **Rosacea** (formerly acne rosacea) is considered a medical disorder (diagnosed by a dermatologist), and is characterized by redness/flushing, dilated blood vessels (telangiectasias), distended capillaries (couperose), and – in some cases – papules (pimples) and pustules (pimples with pus).

- **Alipidic skin** (AKA **dry skin**) doesn't produce enough sebum (indicated by an absence of visible pores). It becomes dehydrated (i.e. lacks moisture), and may look flaky or dry, with fine lines and wrinkles. It may also feel itchy or tight. It is treated by using hydrators that bind water to the skin's surface.

Disorders of the sudoriferous (sweat) glands

- **Anhidrosis** is the inability to sweat – often a result of damage to autonomic nerves. It can be life-threatening and needs medical attention.

- **Bromhidrosis** is foul-smelling perspiration. There are several treatments, including over-the-counter preparations,

Botox injections, and the use of lasers on the sweat glands.

- **Hyperhidrosis** is excessive sweating, caused by heat or general body weakness. It requires a medical referral.

- **Miliaria rubra** (AKA **prickly heat**) is an acute inflammatory disorder of the sweat glands, caused by exposure to excessive heat. It's characterized by the eruption of small, red cysts and burning, itching skin, and it usually clears quickly without treatment.

Other skin types, disorders, inflammations, and common infections (that you may be tested on)

- **Hyperpigmentation** (dark blotches of color) is usually caused by sun exposure or hormone imbalances. It can be treated with mild exfoliation and home care products that discourage pigmentation.

- **Leukoderma** is a skin disorder that produces light, abnormal patches (hypopigmentation) – usually caused by a burn, scar, inflammation, or congenital disease that destroys the pigment-producing cells. Vitiligo and albinism are two forms of hypopigmentation. Vitiligo is characterized by patches of skin that have lost their pigment, whereas albinism affects the entire body.

  ("**Leuko**" is from the Greek language meaning "white".)

- **Sensitive skin** will look "thin" and is easily inflamed. It is treated by avoiding strong fragrances or strong exfoliating products.

70

- **Dermatitis** is a broad term that describes any inflammatory condition of the skin.

- A **cicatrix** is a **scar** – i.e. a slightly raised or depressed area of the skin that forms as a result of the healing process (after an injury or lesion).

- **Keloids** are a type of raised scar, resulting from the excessive growth of fibrous/scar tissue where the skin has healed after an injury. Keloids will form along any type of scar for people susceptible to them.

- **Lentigines** are freckles.

- **Verrucas** (AKA **warts**) are caused by a virus or infection. They're very contagious.
  .

- **Fissures** are cracks in the skin that penetrate the derma (such as chapping on hands or lips).

Skin cancer

There are three types of skin cancer:

- **Basal cell carcinoma** is the most common and least severe type. It is characterized by light/pearly nodules and has a 90% survival rate (if diagnosed and treated early).

- **Squamous cell carcinoma** is characterized by scaly red papules/nodules. Survival rates depend on the stage of diagnosis.

- **Malignant melanoma** is the least common (5% of all diagnoses) but most dangerous form. It is characterized by black/dark brown patches on the skin that may be uneven in texture, jagged, or raised. It is 100% fatal if left untreated, but has a good survival rate if detected early (94% five-year survival rate).

Basics of electricity

Understanding electrotherapy

Electrotherapy is the use of electrical currents to treat the skin.

An **electrode** (AKA **probe**) is an applicator for directing electric current from an electrotherapy device to the client's skin.

Modalities are the currents used in electrical facial and scalp treatments. Each modality has a different effect on the skin.

Each modality needs two electrodes – a negative (cathode) and a positive (anode) – to conduct the flow of electricity through the body. There's one exception to this rule: the Tesla high-frequency current (more on this later).

Modalities

There are three main modalities used in cosmetology:

1: Galvanic current is a constant and a direct current. It produces chemical changes when it passes through the tissues and fluids of the body, which provides cosmetologists with many different uses – including: infusing water-soluble products into unbroken skin; infusing an acidic or alkaline product into deeper tissue; and softening/emulsifying grease deposits and blackheads in the hair follicle – to treat acne, milia, and comedones.

2: Microcurrent is a type of galvanic treatment that uses a very low level of electrical current. It doesn't travel through the entire body; instead, it serves only the specific area being treated.

It can be used in many ways, but is best known for helping to tone the skin in order to produce a lifting effect for aging skin that lacks elasticity. It can also improve blood and lymph circulation, open and close hair follicles and pores, reduce redness/inflammation, and minimize healing time for acne lesions.

3: Tesla current (AKA **high-frequency current** or **violet ray**) is a thermal or heat-producing current with a high rate of oscillation or vibration in which only one electrode is used to perform the service. It doesn't produce muscle contractions, and works by warming tissues, which allows for better absorption of various treatment products.

It stimulates blood circulation, increases skin metabolism, and relieves congestion. It can also be applied after extraction or during treatments for acne-prone skin, thanks to its germicidal effect.

Physical mixtures

Physical mixtures are physical combinations/blends of matter in any proportions. For example, salt water is a physical mixture of salt and water in any proportion. The properties of a physical mixture are the combined properties of the substances in the mixture. Most of the products used by cosmetologists are physical mixtures.

If something isn't a physical mixture, it's a "pure substance" instead – which is a chemical combination of matter in fixed proportions. For example, distilled water is a pure substance consisting of two atoms of hydrogen and one atom of oxygen in fixed proportions. Pure substances have their own unique properties – i.e. properties that are different from simply combining the properties of the substance in the mixture.)

Solutions, **suspensions**, and **emulsions** are all physical mixtures.

Surfactants

A surfactant (meaning "surface active agent") is a type of emulsifier. It's an ingredient that allows otherwise-incompatible ingredients – such as oil and water – to stabilize rather than separate into layers.

It also stirs up activity on any surface being cleaned to help trap dirt and remove it from the surface.

Surfactants provide a number of uses in skin care and cosmetics:

- **As a detergent for cleansing (e.g. skin cleansers and shampoo)**

- As a wetting agent in perms
- **As a foaming agent (e.g. in shampoo and foaming skin cleansers)**
- **As an emulsifier in creams and lotions**
- As a conditioning agent in skin care and hair care products
- As a solubilizer for perfumes and flavors

How surfactants work

A surfactant molecule has two important parts:

- The head of the surfactant is "**hydrophilic**", which means it attracts or combines with water.
- The tail is "**lipophilic**", which means it likes to combine with fats and oils.

When a surfactant is dissolved in an oil-and-water substance, the hydrophilic head dissolves in the water while the lipophilic tale dissolves in the oil, temporarily joining them together to form an emulsion.

Note: "lipophilic" (which attracts fats/oils) is often used interchangeably with "hydrophobic" (which means "repelled by water"), while "hydrophilic" (which attracts water) is often used interchangeably with "lipophobic" (which means "repelled by fats/oils"). These terms aren't synonymous, but they're often used as if they are – so be aware if you get any questions about hydrophobic or lipophobic substances.

The pH scale

A pH scale is a measure of the acidity and alkalinity of a substance. It has a range of 0 to 14:

- A pH below 7 is an acidic solution. (The lower the number, the more acidic the solution.)
- A pH of 7 is a neutral solution.
- A pH above 7 is an alkaline solution. (The higher the number, the more alkaline the solution.)

Only substances that contain water can have a pH.

The pH scale is a logarithmic scale. "Logarithm" means "multiples of 10". This means that a change of one whole number on the pH scale represents a tenfold change in pH. For example, a PH of 9 is 10 times more alkaline than a PH of 8. A change of two whole numbers represents a change of "10 times 10" (that is, a 100-fold change). So a pH of 9 is 100 times more alkaline than a pH of 7.

The pH scale measures hydrogen ions and hydroxide ions in a substance.

- The hydrogen ion is acidic. The more hydrogen ions there are in a substance, the more acidic it will be.
- The hydroxide ion is alkaline. The more hydroxide ions there are in a substance, the more alkaline it will be.

Pure (distilled water) contains the same number of hydrogen ions as hydroxide ions, so it has a pH of 7 (neutral).

Although pure water is neutral on the pH scale, it is 100 times more alkaline than your hair and skin (which have a pH between 4.5 and

5.5). This is why pure water can cause the hair to swell by as much as 20% (which is what alkaline substances do – see below), and why water is drying to the skin.

As acidity increases, alkalinity decreases – and vice versa.

Even the strongest acid will contain *some* alkalinity – and vice versa.

When the skin is exposed to extremes in pH levels (e.g. pH 3), extreme dryness can occur.

Acids and alkalis in the salon

Acids

- **Alpha hydroxy acids (AHAs)** are derived from plants (mostly fruit). They're used in salons to exfoliate the skin and to help adjust the pH of a lotion/cream.
- **Thioglycolic acid** works to contract and harden hair. It has a strong, unpleasant smell and is used when creating permanent waves.
- **Acid solutions in general** will contract/shrink and harden hair. It's for this reason that shampoos for color-treated hair are always acidic: they close the cuticle and prevent color-fading.

Alkalis

- **Alkalis** (AKA **bases**) soften and swell hair, callused skin, the cuticle on the nail plate, and skin. Note: the words "alkali" and "base" are interchangeable.
- **Sodium hydroxide** (AKA **lye**) is very strong, and is used in chemical hair relaxers and callus softeners. These products should not touch or sit on the skin as they may cause a

burning sensation. Always wear safety glasses to avoid eye contact.

Acids + alkalis in equal proportions

When acids and alkalis are mixed together in equal proportions, they neutralize each other to form pure water.

- **Neutralizing shampoos** work by creating an acid-alkali neutralization reaction.
- **Normalizing lotions** (used to neutralize hair relaxers) do the same.
- **Liquid soaps** are normally slightly acidic, and they can neutralize alkaline callus softener residues left on the skin after rinsing.

Hair Care and Services

Structure of the hair

Trichology is the name given to the scientific study of hair, its diseases, and its care.

A mature strand of human hair is divided into two parts:

- The **hair root** is located below the surface of the epidermis (the outer layer of the skin).
- The **hair shaft** projects above the epidermis.

The five main structures of the hair root

The hair root contains **hair follicles**, the hair bulb, the dermal **papilla**, the arrector pili muscle, and **sebaceous glands**.

- **Hair follicles** are distributed all over the body – not just the scalp. (The only exceptions are the palms of the hands and the soles of the foot.) Follicles are tube-like pockets/depressions in the skin that contain the hair root, which is where the hair grows from.

- **Sebaceous glands** (AKA **oil glands**) sit in the skin. They are connected to the hair follicles and secrete a fatty/oily substance called sebum, which lubricates the skin and maintains the softness of the hair. (**Sebaceous glands are glands of excretion**.)

- When the **dermal papilla** is damaged, hair growth will be inhibited.

The three main layers of the hair shaft

The three main layers are the **hair cuticle**, the **cortex**, and the **medulla**.

- The **cuticle** is the outermost layer, and it provides a barrier to protect the inner structure of the hair. It is responsible for creating the shiny, smooth, silky feeling of healthy hair.

- The **cortex** is the middle layer, and both the elasticity of the hair and its natural color are the result of particular protein structures found in the cortex called **side bonds**. These protein structures must be broken or stretched for services such as wet setting, hair coloring, permanent waving, thermal styling, and chemical hair relaxing to take place. (Broken bonds will reform at the end of the process through a variety of different processes.)

- The **medulla** is the innermost layer. Generally, only thick, coarse hair contains a medulla (and it's entirely possible for very fine and naturally blond hair to lack a medulla completely). The medulla is not involved in salon services.

Hair pigment

The cortex contains the pigments that make up a person's natural hair color. As you'll know from the section on skin color, these tiny grains of pigment are called melanin, and there are two types of melanin:

- **Eumelanin** is a dark brown to black pigment. A lower concentration of eumelanin will produce brown hair.
- **Pheomelanin** is a red and/or yellow pigment. (A larger concentration will produce red hair, whereas a lower concentration will produce blond hair.)

All natural hair color is the result of the ratio of eumelanin to pheomelanin (as well as the total number and size of the pigment granules).

The two main types of hair

There are two main types of hair found on the body:

- **Vellus hair** (AKA **lanugo hair**) is short, fine, unpigmented, and downy. It is usually found in areas of the body that are normally considered hairless (such as the forehead, eyelids, and bald scalp), as well as all the other areas of the body – apart from the palms of the hands or soles of the feet, which genuinely are hairless.

  Vellus hair helps with the evaporation of perspiration, and it almost never has a medulla.

- **Terminal hair** is long, coarse, and pigmented (with the exception of gray hair), and it appears on the scalp, legs, arms, and body. It usually has a medulla.

Much vellus hair becomes terminal hair (e.g. on the male chest, face, legs, arms, and feet) during puberty. All hair follicles are able to produce either vellus or terminal hair, depending on genetics, age, and hormones.

Growth cycles of hair

Hair growth occurs in cycles, and each cycle has three phases that are repeated over and over throughout a person's life. Each cycle lasts around four to five years (on average). The three phases are:

Phase 1: the anagen phase (often referred to as the "growth" phase), when new hair is produced through a process called **keratinization**.

Keratinization is when newly formed cells start to travel upward through the hair follicle. As they mature, they fill up with a fibrous protein called keratin and continue to move upward as they lose their nucleus and die. By the time the hair shaft emerges from the scalp, the cells of the hair are completely keratinized and are no longer living. The hair shaft that emerges is therefore a nonliving fiber composed of keratinized protein. (Hair is approximately 90% protein.)

The typical growth cycle is three to five years, and the average growth is about 0.5 inches (1.25 centimeters) per month – although the rate of growth varies on different parts of the body, between sexes, and with age. About 90% of hair is in this phase at any one time.

Note: the anagen phase should not be confused with "androgens", which are a type of hormone.

Phase 2: the catagen phase (often referred to as the "transition" phase), which is the brief transition period (1–2 weeks) between the growth and resting phases of the hair follicle.

The follicle canal shrinks to about 1/6th its original length and detaches from the surface of the skin, the hair bulb disappears, the shrunken root end forms the shape of a rounded club, and no pigment is produced. Less than 1% of hair is in the catagen phase at any time.

Phase 3: the telogen phase (often referred to as the "resting" phase), which is the final phase of the growth cycle, and lasts 3–6 months. About 10% of hair is in this phase at any point. The hair is either shed during this phase or it remains in place until the next anagen phase – when the new hair growing pushes it out.

Normal hair loss

Hair undergoes a continuous growth, fall, and replacement of individual hair strands daily. A hair that is shed during the telogen phase is replaced by a new hair, in the same follicle, in the next anagen phase.

The average person loses 35 to 40 strands per day.

Abnormal hair loss

Abnormal hair loss is called **alopecia**. The three most common types of abnormal hair loss are:

- **Androgenic/androgenetic alopecia (commonly referred to as "male pattern baldness")** is when terminal hair "miniaturizes" back into vellus hair. By the age of 35, about 40% of both women and men will show some degree of hair loss.

- **Alopecia areata** is an autoimmune disorder that leads to hair loss in patches – and can eventually lead to hair loss across the entire head.

- **Postpartum alopecia** is hair loss that occurs toward the end of pregnancy or soon after delivery. It almost always grows back.

Disorders of the hair

- **Canities** is the technical term for gray hair (although the hair can actually be anywhere between white and gray), and it's caused by the loss of the hair's natural melanin pigment. The loss may be congenital (albinos) or acquired (age, illness, or anxiety). Other than the absence of pigment, gray hair is exactly the same as pigmented hair: it is not coarser or more resistant.

- **Ringed hair** is a variety of canities characterized by alternating bands of gray and pigmented hair throughout the length of the hair strand.

- **Hypertrichosis** (AKA **hirsuties**) is where terminal hair grows in areas that normally grow only vellus hair. Examples include mustaches or beards on women.

- **Trichoptilosis** is the technical term for split ends, which can only be removed by cutting them off.

- **Fragilitas crinium** is brittle hair, which means the hair can split at any point along its length. Treatment includes conditioning (to avoid the hair splitting in the first place) and haircutting above a split to avoid further damage.

- **Trichorrhexis nodosa** (AKA **knotted hair**) is characterized by brittleness and the formation of nodular swellings along the hair shaft. Treatment involves softening the hair with conditioners and moisturizers.

Disorders of the scalp

Pityriasis

Pityriasis is the technical term for **dandruff**, which is characterized by the excessive production and accumulation of skin cells. Whereas tiny individual skin cells are normally shed one at a time, dandruff involves shedding an accumulation of large, visible clumps of skin cells instead.

It's believed that dandruff is caused by "**malassezia**": a naturally occurring fungus that is present on all human skin but causes the symptoms of dandruff when it grows out of control. Anti-dandruff scalp shampoos contain antifungal agents that suppress the growth of malassezia.

There are two main types of dandruff:

- **Pityriasis capitis simplex** (AKA **dandruff**) is characterized by scalp irritation, large flakes of epidermis ("scales"), and an itchy scalp. The scales will scatter loosely in the hair, fall to the shoulders, or may attach to the scalp in clumps. Treatment involves using anti-dandruff shampoos, conditioners, and topical lotions. (A client with dandruff can still have their appointment in the salon: they do not need to be referred elsewhere.)

- **Pityriasis steatoides** is a more severe case of dandruff. It consists of an accumulation of waxy or greasy scales, mixed with sebum, that stick to the scalp in crusts. When accompanied by redness and inflammation, it's called **seborrheic dermatitis** – which can also be found in the eyebrows and beard. You shouldn't perform a service on someone with either of these conditions – and they must be referred to a physician.

Tinea

Tinea, which is the technical term for ringworm – a highly contagious fungal infection (which is a type of microscopic plant parasite and NOT an animal parasite, as the word "worm" suggests). It is characterized by itching, scales, and occasionally painful circular lesions. To help prevent the spread of this disease in the salon, you must follow approved cleaning and disinfection procedures. You shouldn't treat anyone with tinea, and they must be referred to a physician for medical treatment.

Here are some of the main forms of tinea:

- **Tinea pedis** (AKA **athlete's foot**) causes itchy red skin – usually on the bottom of the foot/feet, between the fourth and fifth toes.
- **Tinea capitis** is a fungal infection (i.e. a plant parasite) of the scalp, where red spots are seen at the opening of the hair follicles and the hair becomes brittle. Like other forms of tinea, it can be spread easily to a non-infected area or person by means of improperly disinfected tools.
- **Tinea barbae** (AKA **barber's itch**) is the most frequently encountered fungal infection resulting from hair services – and it looks like tinea capitis.

Parasitic infections

Parasitic infections are highly contagious. (Parasites are organisms that grow, feed, and take shelter on other living matter, while contributing nothing to the survival of the host.)
To help prevent spreading parasitic infections in the salon, you must follow approved cleaning and disinfection procedures. You shouldn't treat anyone with a parasitic infection, and they must be referred to a physician for medical treatment.

There are two main types of parasitic infection: scabies and lice.

Scabies

Scabies is caused by a parasite called a mite that burrows under the skin. Blisters ("vesicles") and inflamed pimples with pus ("pustules") appear on the scalp from the irritation caused by the parasite.

Pediculosis capitis (AKA **head lice**; "caput" means "head") is when head lice infest the hair and scalp and start to feed on the scalp, causing it to itch. If the scalp is scratched, it can cause an infection. Head lice are transmitted between people by sharing hats, brushes, combs, and other personal articles.

As these parasites feed on the scalp, it begins to itch. If the scalp is scratched, it can cause an infection. Head lice are transmitted from one person to another by contact with infested hats, combs, brushes, and other personal articles. You can distinguish head lice from dandruff flakes by looking closely at the scalp with a magnifying glass.

You should not perform a service on anyone with pediculosis; they must be referred to a physician or pharmacist. Several nonprescription medications are available.

Bacterial infections

Bacterial infections of the scalp are caused by two strains of bacteria known as staphylococci and streptococci. The most common types of staphylococci are:

- **Furuncles**, which are boils: localized bacterial infections of the hair follicle).
- **Carbuncles**, which are inflammations of the subcutaneous tissue caused by staphylococci – similar to furuncles but larger.

- **Folliculitis** (AKA **barber's itch** or **hot tub folliculitis**), which is an infection of the hair follicles frequently caused by staphylococcus or other bacteria.

Hair and scalp analysis

Because different types of hair react differently to the same service, all salon services must begin with an analysis of the client's scalp and hair type.

The four most important factors to consider are texture, density, porosity, and elasticity. Also important are growth pattern and dryness vs oiliness.

Note: the exam board NEVER refers to a hair's "thickness" or "thinness". Instead, it always refers to its "texture" and "density".

Hair texture

Hair texture is the thickness/diameter of the individual hair strand (determined by feeling a single dry strand between the fingers), and it can be classified as **coarse, medium, or fine**. Hair texture can vary from strand to strand on the same person's head. Coarse hair has the largest diameter, and is the strongest. It may require more processing than medium or fine hair. Medium hair is the most common and poses no special concerns/problems. Fine hair has the smallest diameter and is easiest to process. It is also more fragile and susceptible to damage.

When it comes to styling, coarse hair tends to stick out if it is cut too short. Fine hair can be cut to very short lengths and will still lie flat. If, however, a client has fine (texture) but thin (density) hair, cutting too short can result in the scalp showing through.

Hair density

Hair density measures the number of individual hair strands on 1 square inch (2.5 square centimeters) of scalp, which gives an indication of how many hairs there are on a person's head. Hair density can be classified as low, medium, or high (or thin, medium, or thick/dense).

People with the same hair texture can have different densities, and people with the same hair density can have different textures.

Hair porosity

Hair porosity refers to the ability of the hair to absorb moisture, liquids, or chemicals. The degree of porosity is directly related to the condition of the cuticle layer:

Hair with poor/low porosity is healthy hair. It has a compact/closed cuticle layer and resists being penetrated by moisture (it is "hydrophobic"). Note: there is no such thing as "bad porosity".
Hair with poor/low porosity hair requires an alkaline solution to raise/open/soften the cuticle and allow uniform saturation/processing.

Coarse hair normally has poor/low porosity, but this isn't always the case.

Hair with good/high porosity has a raised (open) cuticle layer that easily absorbs moisture (it is "hydrophilic"). When hair colors are applied, they'll absorb much faster but will also fade much more quickly.

Hair with good/high porosity is considered to be *overly* porous – often due to previous overprocessing. This type of hair is often damaged, fragile, dry, and brittle. You'll need to use chemical solutions that have a lower pH (i.e. are less alkaline), to harden/shrink/close the cuticle, reduce porosity, and help prevent further overprocessing/damage.

Fine hair normally has good/high porosity (although this isn't always the case).

Hair with average porosity is where the cuticle is slightly raised and accepts color products easily (but not too easily!). This is considered normal hair. When chemical services are performed on hair with average porosity, no special treatment is required.

Hair elasticity

Hair elasticity is the ability of the hair to stretch and return to its original length without breaking. This "stretch test" is often referred to as the "pull test".

Hair elasticity is determined by the strength of the hair's "side bonds" (chains of proteins found in the cortex/middle layer of the hair – see earlier). Hair with low elasticity is brittle and breaks easily – and it may not be able to hold the curl from wet setting, permanent waving, or thermal styling. When chemical services are performed on hair with low elasticity, a milder solution with a lower (i.e. less alkaline) pH is required to prevent additional processing and minimize further damage.

Hair growth patterns

There can be multiple **hair growth patterns** (AKA the **natural fall, natural part** or **natural falling position**) on one head of hair, and it's important to consider them all when creating a haircut or hairstyle. Certain types of growth pattern affect where the hair ends up once dry, so you may need to use less tension when cutting these areas to compensate. The main types of growth pattern are:

- A **hair stream** is hair that flows in the same direction, resulting from follicles sloping in the same direction. "Normal" hair consists of two streams flowing in opposite directions from the head to form a natural parting.
- A **whorl** is hair that forms in a circular pattern (such as on the crown of the head).
- A **cowlick** is a tuft of hair that stands up straight. It's usually more noticeable at the front hairline (the hair that grows at the outermost perimeter along the face), but can be found anywhere on the head.

Dry v Oily

Dry hair/scalp is caused by inactive sebaceous glands. Excessive shampooing or dry climates aggravate the dryness further, and the condition should be treated with products that contain moisturizers and emollients. **Oily hair/scalp** is caused by overactive sebaceous glands or improper shampooing, and can be treated by properly washing with a normalizing shampoo (plus a balanced diet, exercise, regular shampooing, and good personal hygiene).

Principles of hair design

There are five important principles in art and design, which are also the basis of hair design:

- **Proportion** is the comparative relationship of one thing to another.
- **Balance** is establishing equal or appropriate proportions to create symmetry.
- **Rhythm** is a regular pulsation or recurrent pattern of movement. An example of fast rhythm in hair design is tight curls (a slow rhythm would be larger shapes or long waves).
- **Emphasis** (AKA **focus**) is an area of emphasis or focus to draw the eye to it. E.g. wave patterns, color, change in form, or ornamentation.
- **Harmony** holds all the other elements of the design together.

Hair brushing, shampooing, conditioning, scalp care, and draping

The two basic requirements for a healthy scalp are:

- Cleanliness
- Stimulation

Hair brushing

Correct hair brushing helps to:

- Stimulate blood circulation to the scalp
- Remove dust, dirt, and hairspray buildup from the hair
- Give the hair added shine

A brush with natural bristles is most suitable for regular hair brushing use.

Always begin brushing the hair from the ends first and then work up toward the scalp. You can then freely brush the hair in order to remove all tangles. When brushing wet hair, use a wide-toothed comb instead.

Shampooing and pH scales

As explained in "Scientific Concepts", the pH scale ranges from 0 to 14.

- The more acidic a substance (i.e. the more hydrogen ions it contains), the smaller the number.
- The more alkaline the substance (i.e. the more hydroxide ions it contains), the higher the number.
- A completely neutral substance (which contains the same number of hydrogen ions as hydroxide ions) has a pH of 7. Distilled water has a pH of 7.

Understanding pH levels will help you select the correct shampoo for your client.

- Hair and skin have a natural pH of 5 – i.e. more acidic than "neutral".
- An alkaline shampoo will have a pH of 7.1 or higher. The more alkaline the shampoo, the stronger and harsher it will be. It can leave the hair dry, brittle and porous – and hair with a high porosity can lead to faster fading in color-treated hair. The benefit of alkaline shampoos is that they cause the hair to soften and swell, causing the cuticle layer to open – which allows the shampoo to be absorbed well.

- An acidic shampoo will have a PH ranging from 0 to 6.9. A slightly acidic shampoo more closely matches the ideal pH of hair.

Types of shampoo

- **pH-balanced shampoo** is balanced to the pH of the skin and hair (4.5 to 5.5) by adding citric, lactic, or phosphoric acid to the shampoo. A pH-balanced shampoo prevents excessive dryness and hair damage. It helps to close the hair cuticle, and is recommended for hair that's been color-treated/lightened.
- **Conditioning/moisturizing shampoo** makes the hair appear smooth and shiny, and improves its manageability. Protein and biotin are two examples of conditioning agents added to these shampoos. They are also nonstripping, which means they don't remove artificial color from the hair.
- **Medicated shampoo** reduces dandruff and other scalp conditions. It can be quite strong and may affect the color of color-treated/lightened hair. In some cases it must remain on the scalp for a longer period of time than regular shampoo. (Note: anti-dandruff scalp shampoos contain antifungal agents that suppress the growth of malassezia. See earlier for more on this)
- **Clarifying shampoo** contains an active chelating agent that binds to metals (e.g. iron and copper) and removes them from the hair. It also enriches hair, helps retain moisture, and makes hair more manageable. It should be used when buildup is evident, before chemical services, and after swimming.

Note: sometimes, a client's health means a wet shampoo will be uncomfortable. E.g. an elderly client may be uncomfortable at the shampoo bowl due to pressure at the back of the neck. In such cases, you can use a **dry shampoo** (AKA **powder shampoo**) instead.

Shampoo and surfactants

After water, the second most common ingredient in shampoos is the **surfactant**. As we know from "Scientific Concepts", a surfactant is a substance that allows oil and water to mix/emulsify. A surfactant molecule has two ends: the hydrophilic (water-attracting) head, and the lipophilic (oil/fat-attracting) tail.

While shampooing, the hydrophilic head attracts water, while the lipophilic tail attracts oil. This creases a push-pull process that causes the oils and dirt to be rolled up into little balls that can be lifted off the hair in the water and rinsed off.

Soft water vs hard water for shampooing

Soft water (rainwater or chemically softened water) contains only small amounts of minerals, and it therefore allows soap and shampoo to lather freely – making it preferable for shampooing. Hard water (usually well water) contains minerals that reduce the ability of soap or shampoo to lather, and may also change the results of the haircoloring service. A water treatment process can be used to soften hard water.

Types of conditioner

Conditioner is applied to hair to give it more moisture and protein. While it cannot improve the quality of new hair growth, it can restore shine, manageability, luster, and strength to dry/damaged hair until it grows long enough to be cut off and replaced with new, healthier hair.

There are three main types of conditioner:

- **Rinse-out conditioner**, which is rinsed out of the hair after being worked through the hair.
- **Treatment or repair conditioner** (AKA **deep-conditioning treatment**), which is deep and penetrating to restore protein and moisture (often requires more time on the hair or the application of heat). If conditioner is to remain on the hair for more than a minute, place a plastic cap on the client's head and sit them upright for the recommended time.
- **Leave-in conditioner**, which isn't rinsed out.

Among other ingredients, most conditioners contain **silicone** (to reflect light and make the hair appear shiny) and **humectants** – which are moisture-binding substances that promote the retention of moisture.

Most treatment conditioners and leave-in conditioners contain proteins. These conditioners are also known as **moisturizing or protein conditioners**, and they are designed to penetrate the cortex and reinforce the hair shaft from within to temporarily reconstruct the hair. They also contain humectants that attract moisture from the hair and are absorbed into the cortex.

Scalp care

Scalp treatments and massage can be performed at two different points in the hair service:

- If a scalp condition is present, the massage can be performed before a shampoo (as a treatment massage).
- If the primary purpose is relaxation, the massage can be performed during the shampoo.

101

The difference between a relaxation and treatment massage is the products you use.

Note: scalp massage should not be performed on clients with hypertension.

Draping

After the client consultation and before any cosmetology service can begin, the client must be appropriately draped for whichever service(s) they're about to receive. Draping protects the client's clothing from water, hair color, and so on.

Before draping, always do the following:

- Ask the client to remove any necklaces.
- Wash your hands.
- Turn the client's collar in.

There are two types of draping in a salon:

Shampoo (wet) draping

Shampoo (wet) draping is for any service that involves either shampoo + styling or shampoo + haircutting. Conditioner might also be used.

Use two terry towels: one under the cape and one over. Before cutting/styling, these should be replaced with a neck strip – which is secured with a haircutting or styling cape. Fold the neck strip down so that no part of the cape touches the client's skin.

Chemical service draping is for clients who will have a chemical service/treatment and who will *not* have a shampoo before the service.

Use two terry towels again – one under the cape and one over. These should remain in place until the service is complete, and must be regularly checked for dryness. (Replace if they become wet or soiled.)

If the instructions on a particular chemical product state that shampooing must take place *first,* follow the procedure for shampoo draping, then re-drape for a chemical service.

Note: as you'll see above, **draping is the same for both shampoo and chemical services**. The only difference is the timing of when the towels are removed.

Basic principles of haircutting

Lines and angles

Every haircut is made up of lines and angles:

- An **angle** is the space between two lines/surfaces that intersect at a given point.
- A **line** is a continuous mark used as a guide, to make the hair fall into a particular shape.

Sections and subsections

To maintain control during haircutting, hair is divided into uniform working areas called **sections** (and each section can be further divided into **subsections**).

Elevation

To achieve certain hairstyles, subsections of hair must be lifted/held away from the head at a certain angle before being cut. The angle/degree at which the subsection is held is known as the **elevation** (AKA **projection** or **lifting**). Elevation occurs when you lift any section of hair above 0 degrees (where 0 degrees involves *not* lifting the hair at all, and simply cutting length off the hair at the bottom). If a haircut is not a single length, elevation will have been used.

- A **graduated haircut** is a slow or immediate buildup of weight at a low to medium elevation (usually 45 degrees). Other ways to create a graduated haircut are by cutting with tension or over direction.
- A **layered haircut** is when the hair is elevated 90 degrees or higher, which removes weight. Types of layered haircut include the **pixie**, **cro**, **Caesar**, and **shag**.
- A **blunt**, one-length haircut has no elevation (i.e. 0 degrees). The blunt haircut is also known as a **bob**, **one-length**, or **pageboy** haircut.

The most commonly used elevations are:

- 45 degrees
- 90 degrees

Bear in mind...

- Hair length is also a factor in the end result: the weight of longer hair means it often appears heavier or less layered – even if it's received more elevation.
- Curly hair will need less elevation or be kept a bit longer compared to straighter hair, because of shrinkage.

Over direction

Over direction involves lifting the hair and cutting it above the head to create extra body and volume. Whereas elevation is the degree to which you lift a subsection of hair away from the head, over direction involves combing the hair away from its natural falling position (rather than straight out from the head). This technique is mainly used in graduated and layered haircuts.

Cutting line

The **cutting line** (AKA **cutting position, cutting angle, finger angle**, and **finger position**) is the angle at which a stylist holds their fingers when cutting, to create the end shape of the hair. There are four main types of cutting line:

- A **horizontal cutting line** is used when creating a blunt (one length) haircut. (It's customary to cut below your fingers or on the inside of your knuckles for such a haircut.)
- A **vertical cutting line** (AKA **90-degree cutting line**) creates a layered shape.
- A **diagonal cutting line** (AKA **45-degree cutting line**) creates styles like a graduated bob.

Weight line

The **weight line** is the part of the haircut that holds the most weight. (It's where the ends of the hair hang together.) Think of it as the "base".

Guidelines / guides

In haircutting, a **guideline** (or **guide**) is a section of hair that determines the length of the hair will be when cut. It's normally the first section cut when creating a shape.

Guidelines are located either at the **perimeter** (the outer line, which starts at the forehead, goes down past the ears to the nape of the neck, and back again) or inside the haircut rather than on the perimeter (known as an **interior guideline**).

There are two types of guideline: **stationary** and **traveling**.

- A **stationary guideline** is used to create a blunt (one length) haircut, or in a haircut that uses over direction to create an increase in length or weight.

  A stationary guideline does not move. All other sections are combed to the stationary guideline and cut at the same angle and length.

- A **traveling (or movable) guideline** is used to create a layered or graduated haircut.

  A traveling guideline travels with you as you work through the haircut: you take a small slice of the previous subsection and move it to the next subsection (or position), where it becomes your new guideline.

Tension

Tension is the amount of pressure applied when combing and holding a subsection; it is created by stretching or pulling the subsection.

With curly or wavy hair, less tension is better: a lot of tension will lead to the hair shrinking even more than usual as it dries. It's also best to use less tension around the ears and on hairlines with strong growth patterns.

Client consultation

The client consultation is the conversation between you and your client when you discover what kind they want out of their haircut, offer suggestions and advice, and reach a joint decision about the most suitable haircut.

In addition to asking questions about your client's natural hair, lifestyle, and requirements when it comes to her hairstyle, the consultation should also involve:

- Analyzing the face shape
- Analyzing the hair

Analyzing the face shape
Triangle/pear-shaped:

- Narrow forehead and wide chin/jaw line.
- A good styling choice is to include a soft fringe (bangs) and height/volume at the top to disguise the narrow forehead.

Oval:

- The forehead is slightly wider than the chin.
- The face is about 1.5 times longer than it is wide at the eyebrows.
- Considered the ideal face shape by artists and photographers.
- This face shape will suit most hairstyles.

Round:

- Round and (usually) wide.
- A good styling choice is to add height/volume at the top and keep the hair close at the sides.

Square:

- Wide at the temples, narrow at the middle third of the face, and squared off at the jaw.
- Bring the shape/silhouette close to the head form. Create volume in the area between the temples and jaw by adding width around the ear area.

Oblong:

- Long and narrow with hollow cheeks.
- A good styling choice is chin length with volume at the sides to give the illusion of width. Keep the hair fairly close to the top of the head.

Diamond:

- Narrow forehead and chin, and a larger width through the cheekbones.

- A good styling choice is one that increases a sense of fullness/width across the jawline and forehead while keeping the hair close to the head at the cheekbone line. Avoid hairstyles that lift away from the cheeks or move back from the hairline on the sides near the ear area.

Inverted triangle (heart-shaped):

- Wide forehead and narrow chin line.
- Style the hair close to the head with no volume. Keep the silhouette at its widest at the jaw and neck area. A bang/fringe is recommended.

Extra considerations:

- Wide-set eyes benefit from a higher half bang to create length in the face.
- Draw attention away from a crooked nose with an asymmetrical, off-center hairstyle.
- For a wide, flat nose, draw the hair away from the face and use a center parting to elongate and narrow the nose.
- Long, narrow noses work best with styles where the hair moves away from the face, creating the illusion of wider facial features.
- For a round jaw, use straight lines at the jaw line.
- For a square jaw, use curved lines at the jaw line.
- A long jaw requires full hair that falls below the jaw line.
- A receding chin works best with hair that's directed forward in the chin area.

Analyzing the hair

As mentioned earlier, four characteristics determine the behavior of hair:

- Growth patterns
- Density
- Texture
- Elasticity

See earlier for information on how these characteristics should influence the hairstyle you create for your client.

It's also important to consider the **wave pattern** – that is, the amount of movement in the hair strand, which varies from client to client (as well as within the same head of hair). Wave patterns refer to the design texture of the hair. A client may have:

- Straight hair (no wave)
- Wavy hair
- Curly hair
- Extremely curly hair
- And anything in between

Haircutting tools

Scissors

Haircutting shears (AKA **scissors**) are mainly used to cut blunt or straight lines of hair.

All professional shears are made of steel – which all have a gauge for "hardness" called the Rockwell hardness. This gauge determines how long the steel can maintain a hard edge before it needs sharpening/maintenance again. Generally, a shear with a Rockwell hardness of 56–57 is ideal (but no higher than 63, as it will be too hard and brittle to work with).

When holding shears, your ring finger should go in the finger grip (ring) of the still blade, and your little finger should be placed on the finger tang (brace). Your thumb should be placed in the finger grip (thumb grip/ring) of the moving blade.

There are a few different types of shear:

- **Texturizing shears** (AKA **thinning shears, tapering* shears, or notching shears**) remove weight/bulk from the hair without shortening the length, and add increased blending.
- **Chunking shears** are useful for taking out big sections.
- **Thinning shears** are the most universally used, providing a consistent reduction of bulk.
- **Blending shears** are great for scissor-over-comb cutting.

Other haircutting tools

- **Razors** (straight or feather blade) are mainly used to create a softer effect on the ends of the hair. Note: razors should not be used on curly hair.
- **Clippers** are mainly used when creating short haircuts, short tapers*, flat tops, and fades. When working with clippers, always work against the direction of the hair growth pattern, especially at the nape. This ensures that you are lifting the hair away from the head and cutting the hair evenly.
- **Trimmers** (AKA **edgers**) are a smaller version of clippers, and they're mainly used on men's haircuts and very short women's haircuts (often to remove unwanted hair at the neckline and around the ears).
- **Sectioning clips** come in a variety of shapes and sizes. The most common types used are jaw/butterfly and duckbill clips.
- A **wide-tooth comb** is for detangling hair.
- A **tail comb** is to create hair sections/subsections.
- A **barber comb** is for close tapers* on the nape and sides when using the scissor-over-comb technique. (The narrow end of the comb allows the shears to get close to the head.)
- A **styling/cutting comb** (AKA **all-purpose comb**) is used in most haircutting procedures. It can be six to eight inches long and has fine teeth at one end and wider teeth at the other. **Note: when combing hair, the two reference points at which the comb leaves the head are the parietal ridge and the occipital bone.**

*A **taper** is when the hair gradually changes from one length to another. The term is used most frequently in barbering, when it generally refers to a "tapered haircut": shorter hair around the perimeter of the haircut, gradually getting longer.

Haircutting techniques

Basic haircuts

There are four basic haircuts on which the art of haircutting is based: blunt, graduated, layered, and long layered. These haircuts make use of the basic principles of haircutting mentioned earlier.

Once you understand these basic haircuts, you can begin experimenting with other cuts and effects.

Blunt haircut (AKA one-length haircut)

- All the hair comes to a single hanging level, forming a weight line.
- Zero elevation.
- Zero over direction.
- Cut with a stationary guide.
- The cutting line can be horizontal, diagonal, or rounded.
- The hair is all cut to one length, which makes it appear thicker. It's therefore an excellent style for finer and thinner hair types.

Graduated haircut (a graduated shape or wedge)

- Where the hair graduates from longer to short (e.g. graduated the back of a bob, or a "forward grad" – layering around the front of the hairstyle). The ends of the hair appear closer together than in a layered style.
- Achieved by cutting the hair with tension.

- Low to medium elevation, or over direction (the most common elevation is 45 degrees). Variations and effects can be created by adjusting the degree of elevation, the amount of over direction, or your cutting line.
- There is a visual buildup of weight in a given area.
- The ends of the hair appear to be stacked.

Layered haircut (a graduated effect)

- Involves cutting shorter pieces of hair that seamlessly fall together to give hair volume and movement. The hair has less weight than graduated haircuts, and the ends appear further apart.
- Cut the hair with elevation (usually 90 degrees and above) or over direction.
- Can use a traveling guide, a stationary guide, or both.
- With a **uniform layered haircut** (a specific type of layered haircut), all hair is elevated to 90 degrees from the scalp and cut at the same length, using an interior traveling guideline (rather than the perimeter) as a guide.

Long layered haircut

- Gives more volume to hairstyles and can be combined with other basic haircuts.
- The resulting shape has shorter layers at the top and increasingly longer layers toward the perimeter.

Hairstyling

The basics of wet hairstyling

These are the wet hairstyling techniques and principles you need to learn and master:

Finger waving

Finger waving is considered to be "the foundation of hairstyling": it teaches you the technique of moving and directing hair, and gives you valuable training in molding hair to the curved surface of the head.

Finger waving involves shaping and directing the hair into an "S" pattern by using fingers, combs, and finger-waving lotion. (Finger-waving lotion – AKA liquid gel – is a type of hair gel that makes the hair pliable to keep it in place during the finger-waving procedure.)

To form the first ridge (which should be on the right side of the head), insert the comb beneath your index finger and pull forward.

Pin curls

Pin curls is the process of making springy and long-lasting curls with good definition and direction. These curls serve as the basis for patterns, lines, waves, rolls, and curls that are used in many hairstyles.

Pin curls are made up of three main parts:

- The **base** is the non-moving part closest to the scalp.
- The **stem** gives the pin curl its direction and movement/mobility.

- The **circle** is the part that's furthest from the scalp. The size of the circle determines the width of the wave and its strength.

Before you begin making pin curls, you need to create your base. There are a few different types of base:

- A **rectangular base** is recommended at the side front hairline for a smooth, upswept effect.
- A **triangular base** helps to prevent breaks or splits in the finished hairstyle. It allows a portion of the hair from each curl to overlap, and is recommended for the front or facial hairline.
- An **arc base** (AKA **half-moon** or **C-shaped**) provides good direction. It can be used at the hairline or in the nape.
- A **square base** can be used on any part of the head, and is suitable for curly hairstyles without much volume or lift.

Roller curls

Rollers (sometimes referred to as "**barrels**") create many of the same effects as pin curls, but they have a few advantages over pin curls:

- They're faster to set the hair (because a roller holds the equivalent of two to four pin curls).
- The hair is wrapped around the roller with tension, providing a stronger and longer-lasting set.
- Rollers come in a variety of shapes, widths, and sizes, which means there are more possibilities for creating different styles.
- The amount of volume achieved depends on the size of the roller and how it sits on its base:
  - The larger the roller, the greater the volume.

116

o   There are three kinds of bases. **On base** (AKA **full base**) creates the most volume; **half base** produces medium volume; **off base** creates the least volume.

Thermal hairstyling

Thermal irons

Thermal waving and curling (AKA **Marcel waving**) involve using thermal irons and various manipulative techniques to wave and curl straight or pressed dry hair. Thermal irons can be electric or stove-heated.

You will need to test thermal irons before use. After heating the iron to the desired temperature, clamp it over a white cloth or a piece of tissue paper for five seconds. If the material scorches or turns brown, the iron is too hot and needs to be left to cool down a bit before using – otherwise it might scorch the hair (and might even discolor white hair).

Thermal pressing combs

Thermal pressing combs are used both to straighten hair and to prepare it for additional services (such as thermal curling and croquignole thermal curling). As with thermal irons, thermal pressing combs can be electric or stove-heated.

Hair straightening (or pressing) is a popular, profitable salon service that temporarily (until the next shampoo) straightens very curly or resistant hair.

Before pressing, you will need to consider the type of hair:

- When pressing **fine hair**, apply less pressure and heat to the hair ends. If the curl form isn't too wiry, you may want to consider flat ironing instead.
- **Short, fine hair** must be given extra care at the hairline, to avoid burns. Also make sure the pressing comb isn't too hot: the hair is fine and will burn easily.
- **Coarse hair** requires enough pressure so that the hair remains straightened.
- **Tinted or lightened hair** may require a conditioning treatment, depending on how damaged it is.
- **Gray hair** may be particularly resistant to pressing. To get good results, use a moderately heated pressing comb with light pressure. Avoid excessive heat as discoloration or breakage can occur.
- **Wiry, curly hair** may be coarse, medium, or fine. It is very resistant to hair pressing and requires more heat and pressing than other types of hair.
- **Coarse, extremely curly hair** is also difficult to press. It requires more heat and pressure than medium or fine hair.

You will need to test pressing combs before use. After heating the comb to the desired temperature, test it on a piece of light paper. If the paper becomes scorched, the comb needs to be left to cool down a bit before using.

Before pressing, you should also prepare the hair by applying a pressing oil or cream – which will condition the hair, help prevent breakage, add sheen, and help hair stay pressed for longer.

Styling long hair

The two basic hairstyles of any "updo" or "half updo"

Updos and half updos are specialty styles for long hair, usually requested by clients for special occasions (weddings, proms, etc.). The following two basic styles are the foundation of every updo:

- The **ponytail** is the foundation for a chignon, bun, and knot (among others), and can be worn in a casual, classic, or trendy style.
- The **French Pleat** can be applied to hair that is longer than shoulder length, and is popular for clients attending formal/elegant functions.

Classic updos

The most common classic updos are the chignon, bun, and twist:
- The **chignon** (AKA the **knot**) is a classic style that's been popular for centuries, and is created out of a simple ponytail. It is usually placed at the crown or the nape. If the client doesn't have naturally straight hair, it will have to be blow dried or pressed straight first.
- The **bun** is also created out of a simple ponytail, and it can sit high or low. The bun can be formed by twisting the hair around the ponytail or back-brushing it and forming it into a bun before securing it with bobby pins.
- The **twist** (AKA the **French pleat**) is an elegant, sleek look that creates a conical-shape look.

Wigs and hairpieces

Wigs

When someone wears a **wig**, their hair is completely concealed or almost completely concealed (80–100% coverage).

There are two basic categories of wigs:

- **Cap wigs** are usually handmade/hand-knotted and require a special fitting. They're made using an elasticized mesh fiber to which the hair is attached, and they have a snug, secure fit. They're a good choice for someone with extremely thin hair or alopecia because the bald won't show through.

- **Capless wigs** (AKA **caps**) are long strips of hair with a threaded edge, which are machine-made from human or artificial hair. The hair is woven into rows of wefts (long strips of hair), which are then sewn to elastic strips in a circular pattern to fit the head shape. Capless wigs are ready to wear, less expensive, lighter, and more comfortable, so they tend to be more popular. They're not a good choice for someone with extremely thin hair or alopecia because you can see through to the scalp.

Cutting and styling wigs
- Cutting a wig is best performed on a wig block or stand. A block is a head-shaped form, usually made of cork or Styrofoam, on which a wig is placed.
- Coloring, perming, relaxing, setting, and basic cut outlining can be performed on a wig block too.

- Combing and finishing a wig should always be done on the client's head.

Hairpieces / hair attachments

If a hair addition doesn't fully cover the hair (as a wig does), it is either a **hairpiece** (a small wig that covers a portion of the top and/or crown of the head, or clips onto another area – such as the nape) or a **hair attachment** of some sort. It usually can't be slept in because it is attached by temporary methods.

There are many different types of hairpieces:

- **Fashion hairpieces** are great for special occasions or as fashion accessories. They're usually constructed on a stiff net base and attached, temporarily, with clips, combs, pins, or elastic.
- **Integration wigs/pieces** have an opening(s) in the base, through which the client's own hair is pulled to blend with the hair of the hairpiece. They're used to add length and/or volume to a client's own hair, and are recommended for those with thinning hair rather than total hair loss (as the scalp is likely to show through).
- **Toupees** are a type of integration wig, and they cover the top and crown of the head. There are two ways to attach them: temporary (tape or clips) or semipermanent (tracks, adhesive, or sewing). Most toupee clients are men, but women can wear them too.
- **Hair extensions** are hair additions that are secured at the base of the client's natural hair to add length, volume, texture, or color. They are either **wefts** (long strips) or **strands** (small bundles, which are attached one by one and are usually pre-bonded or keratin-tipped).

Human hair vs synthetic hair for wigs and hairpieces

Human hair

Human hair looks more realistic, has greater durability, and requires the same styling as natural hair.

However, it also reacts to the climate in the same way that natural hair does. Additionally, color will fade with exposure to light, due to oxidation; it will break and split if mistreated (e.g. by harsh brushing or excessive use of heat); and it needs to be reset after shampooing (which is challenging for someone who aims to maintain the hair at home)

Synthetic hair

Synthetic hair is less expensive than human hair, easy to maintain at home, and doesn't react to the climate in the same way as human hair. What's more, most synthetic wigs, hairpieces, and extensions are already styled (with the cut, color, and texture already set), so they're much quicker than dealing with human hair. Anything made of modacrylic is very strong and durable.

On the downside, it cannot be exposed to extreme heat (such as curling irons, flat irons, hot rollers, or the high heat of blow dryers) – although if it's been coated with a protein base, it might be able to tolerate low heat. And unlike human hair, traditional hair color won't work on it.

How do you tell if a strand of hair is synthetic or real human hair?

The fastest way to tell is to pull the strand out of the wig/hairpiece and burn it with a match. Human hair will burn slowly and give off a distinctive odor. Synthetic hair will either ball up and melt, extinguishing itself, or it will contain to flame and burn out very quickly.

Chemical texture services

Chemical texture services cause a chemical change within the hair's natural wave and curl pattern. They include:

- **Permanent waving**: adding wave or curl to the hair.
- **Relaxing**: removing curl or waves; leaving the hair smooth and straight.
- **Curl re-forming (soft curl permanents)**: loosening overly curly hair.

Importance of pH in texture services

As we know from earlier, the PH scale measures the acidity and alkalinity of a substance by measuring the quantity of hydrogen ions it contains.

- The pH scale has a range from 0 to 14.
- A pH of 7 is neutral.
- A pH below 7 is acidic.
- A pH above7 is alkaline.
- The natural pH of our hair and skin is between 4.5 and 5.5.

Chemical solutions raise the pH of the hair to an alkaline state. When this happens, the hair softens and swells, and the cuticle layer of the hair opens – which allows the solution to reach the middle layer of the hair: the cortex. Note: when hair softens and swells, it also becomes more prone to damage/breakage.

(Brief reminder: the cortex contains protein structures called side bonds that are responsible for the elasticity of the hair and its natural hair color. In order for hair to be colored, waved, chemically relaxed, etc., these protein structures must be broken or stretched.)

Even acid-balanced chemical solutions (of which more later) will raise the alkalinity of the hair. Because these solutions are far less alkaline, however, there will be far less swelling, softening, and opening of the cuticle layer.

Whenever a chemical solution is involved in hairstyling, you should always perform an elasticity test first: hair with low elasticity is brittle and breaks easily – and it may not be able to hold the curl from wet setting, permanent waving, or thermal styling. When chemical services are performed on hair with low elasticity, a milder solution with a lower (i.e. less alkaline) pH is required to prevent additional processing and minimize further damage.

Coarse, resistant hair with a strong, compact cuticle layer will need a highly alkaline chemical solution.

Permanent waving (AKA permanent wrapping or chemical waving)

Permanent waving (AKA **permanent wrapping** or **chemical waving**) is when the hair undergoes two changes:

1. A **physical change** is caused by wrapping the hair on perm rods.
2. The hair then undergoes a **chemical change** when a waving solution and neutralizer are added.

Creating permanent waves is a two-step process involving the use of a reducing/processing agent (i.e. the active ingredient to

124

create the waves) and a neutralizing agent. Some types of permanent wave also require a separate "activator".

Before the service begins, many manufacturers require that you shampoo the client's hair first. If this is the case, drape the client for a shampoo and towel dry the hair until moist. Then re-drape the client for a chemical service.

It's advisable to perform a preliminary test curl on damaged/tinted hair (or where there's uncertainty about the results). The test will help to determine the processing time for optimal curl development, plus the results you can expect to see from the type of solution and tool size/wrapping technique you've selected.

When perming hair that has been tinted, bleached, or highlighted, it is best to use a product that includes a pre-wrap lotion, which helps to equalize porosity.

1: Reducing / processing agents (AKA waving solution)

Reducing/processing agents (AKA **waving solutions**) soften and swell (i.e. expand) the hair, and they open the cuticle, allowing the solution to penetrate into the cortex.

Once in the cortex, the waving solution breaks/stretches a particular kind of side bond in the cortex (called **disulfide bonds**) through a chemical reaction called reduction. A reduction reaction involves either the addition of hydrogen or the removal of oxygen from each of the two sulfur atoms in a disulfide bond. (In permanent waving, it's due to the addition of hydrogen.)

The reduction reaction allows the hair to be waved, colored, etc.

The strength of any permanent wave is based on two factors:
- The concentration of its reducing agent.
- The pH of the solution.

If a weak or low pH solution is used on coarse hair, it may not be able to break the necessary number of disulfide bonds.

Once hair processing is complete, the hair must be rinsed thoroughly for at least five minutes, then each rod must be towel-blotted to remove excess moisture.

2: Neutralizing agents

Neutralizing (often known as "thio neutralization") has two important functions:

- To neutralize/deactivate any waving solution that remains in the hair.
- To rebuild any disulfide bonds that were broken by the waving solution (with the hair now in its new curly form).

The term "neutralizer" is actually inaccurate because the chemical reaction involved is oxidation – using an oxidizer such as hydrogen peroxide (the most common form of neutralizer). Hydrogen peroxide has a pH between 2.5 and 4.5, and it's often abbreviated to **H2O2 (H_2O_2)**, Note: the hydrogen peroxide can sometimes cause the hair to lighten (which can usually be avoided if the hair is thoroughly rinsed and blotted before applying the neutralizer).

(Hydrogen peroxide shouldn't be confused with sodium hydroxide – which is a very strong alkaline (pH 13 or more) used in chemical relaxers.)

The neutralization process normally takes about 5–8 minutes to complete.

Types of permanent wave

Salons offer a variety of permanent wave styles, and it's important to select the right type for each client:

Alkaline waves:

- **Alkaline waves** (AKA **cold waves**) have a **pH between 9.0 and 9.6**.

- **Ammonium thioglycolate (ATG)** is the active ingredient/reducing agent. ATG is an alkaline chemical that's formed when two other chemicals are combined:

    ○ **Thioglycolic acid** (commonly referred to as **thio**).
    ○ **Ammonia,** an alkalizing agent that's added because acids such as thio don't swell the hair or penetrate the cortex.

- Alkaline waves process at room temperature (i.e. "cold wave") without needing any heat.

- Hair should be wrapped with minimal tension because the alkalinity will cause the hair to swell – which puts it at risk of breakage.

- Best for coarse, thick, or resistant hair. Can also be used on naturally curly hair with an uneven curl pattern.

- Note: if a client's hair has previously been treated with a hydroxide relaxer, you must not apply thio to the hair for

127

permanent relaxing or waving: it will not properly relax or curl the hair, and it may cause extreme damage.

Exothermic waves:

- **Exothermic waves** have a **pH between 9.0 and 9.6** (like alkaline waves).

- These waves create their own heat via a reaction when the chemicals mix together. This heat speeds up the processing.

- Best for coarse, thick, or resistant hair.

Ammonia-free waves:

- **Ammonia-free waves** have a **pH between 7.0 and 9.6**.

- They use ingredients called alkanolamines – such as **aminomethylpropanol (AMp)** or **monoethanolamine (MEA)** – instead of ammonia. They don't smell as strong as ammonia, but they can be just as damaging.

- Best for porous to normal hair.

Acid waves:

- The main reducing agent in all acid waves is **glyceryl monothioglycolate (GMTG)**, which has a low pH. Other reducing agents may be included too – such as ATG.

- The pH of natural hair is between 4.5 and 5.5. As a result, the pH of acid waves is still more alkaline than that of hair – which means it still enables the hair to swell (even though the product is considered "acidic" or "neutral" on the pH scale).

- Although the low pH of acid waves may seem like a good thing, repeated exposure to GMTG is known to cause allergic sensitivity in both stylists and clients.

- Also, as with all products that are more alkaline than the hair, there's also the possibility that the hair will be damaged after being permed with true acid waves. (And bear in mind that even the strongest acid also contains some alkalinity.)

- There are two main types of acid waves:

  o **True acid waves** have a **PH between 4.5 and 7,** and they require heat to process. They process more slowly than alkaline waves, and do not produce as firm a curl.

    While some swelling still occurs (see above for the explanation), it is minimal. As a result, the hair must be wrapped with a firm an even tension in order to produce even curls.

    Best for very porous or very damaged hair.

  o **Acid-balanced waves** are an intended compromise between acid waves and alkaline waves: they can be processed at room temperature and will produce a firmer curl, but have a lower pH than alkaline waves (**between 7.8 and 8.2**).

    Most of the acid waves found in today's salons are

actually acid-balanced waves.

Best for porous or damaged hair.

Endothermic waves:

- **Endothermic waves** are activated by an outside heat source (normally a conventional hood-type hairdryer).

- An endothermic chemical reaction is one that absorbs heat from its surroundings.

- Most true acid waves are endothermic.

Selecting the correct perm rod

The types of perm rod are as follows:

- **Concave rods** are the most commonly used perm rod. They have a smaller diameter in the center, which increases to a larger diameter at the ends. They produce a tighter curl in the center, and a looser curl on either side of the strand.

- **Straight rods** are the same diameter along their entire length/curling area, which produces a uniform curl along the entire width of the strand.

- **Loop rods** (AKA **circle rods**) are about 12 inches (30.5 centimeters) long, and they have the same diameter along the entire length of the rod. After the hair is wrapped, the rod is secured by fastening the ends together to form a loop.

- **Soft bender rods** are similar to loop rods, but they have a flexible wire insides that enables them to be bent into almost any shape.

- Today, many clients wish for large, loose curls and waves – which requires the use of **large rollers**, **rag rollers**, and other tools. Larger tools are also used for root perms – where only the base of the hair is permed (to create lift and volume without curl).

End papers (AKA **end wraps**) are absorbent papers that keep the ends of the hair flat and straight when they're being wrapped around perm rods. End papers should always extend beyond the ends of the hair to prevent "fishhooks" (hair that is bent up at the ends).

There are a few common end paper techniques:

- With a **double flat wrap**, one end paper goes under the strand of hair being wrapped, while another end paper goes over. This method provides the most control over the hair ends and keeps them evenly distributed over the entire length of the rod.

- A **single flat wrap** is similar, but there's just one end paper – which goes over the top of the strand being wrapped.

- The **bookend wrap** is the fastest technique, in which one end of paper is folded in half over the hair ends (like an envelope). If not performed correctly, the hair can end up bunched in the fold of the paper, producing an uneven curl.

Sectioning for a perm
- All perm wraps begin by sectioning the hair into **panels**. (The size, shape, and direction of these panels will depend

131

on the wrapping pattern, as well as the type and size of the rod being used.)

- **Base sections** are subsections of panels, and they're usually the length and width of the rod being used. One rod is normally placed on each base section.

- **Base direction** is the angle at which the rod is placed on the head: horizontally, vertically, or diagonally. **Base direction** is also the directional pattern in which the hair is wrapped. Although directional wraps can be wrapped in all directions, bear in mind that wrapping with the natural direction of hair growth causes the least amount of stress to the hair.

Base placement

Base placement refers to the position of the rod in relation to its base section. It is determined by the angle at which the hair is wrapped. Rods can be wrapped **on base**, **half off base**, or **off base**.

- While **on-base placement** (45 degrees beyond perpendicular to its base section) results in greater volume at the scalp area, the extra volume will be lost as soon as the hair starts to grow out. It also causes additional stress and tension, which can mark or break the hair.
- **Half off-base placement** (90 degrees/perpendicular to its base section) minimizes stress and tension on the hair.
- **Off-base placement** (45 degrees below the center of the base section) creates the least amount of volume. It also results in a curl pattern that begins farthest away from the scalp.

Wrapping techniques

When performing a permanent waving service, hair is "wrapped" around a hard roller or rod to create curls and waves. There are two main methods for wrapping hair around the perm rod:

- A **croquignole perm wrap** begins at the ends of the hair, with each layer of hair overlapping the previous layer. Because the hair is wrapped perpendicular to the length of each rod, the diameter of the curl increases with each new layer. **The result is a look that's curlier at the ends and less curly at the roots.**

- A **spiral perm wrap** involves wrapping the hair at an angle, **which results in a curl that's more uniform from the scalp to the ends.** When performed with bender/loop rods, the wrapping is usually from the scalp towards the ends.

Note: these methods apply to a perm wave and ALSO roller setting (wet setting) and thermal styling with hot irons/curling iron.

Wrapping patterns

Different wrapping patterns and types of rod can be combined to create a variety of specialized perm wraps:

- The **basic permanent wrap** (AKA **straight set wrap**) is where all the rods within a panel move in the same direction and are positioned on equal-sized bases. All the base sections are horizontal, and they're the same length and width as the perm rod.
- A **curvature permanent wrap** is where the partings and bases radiate throughout the panels to follow the curvature of the head.

133

- The **bricklay permanent wrap** is where base sections are offset from each other row by row (like the actual technique of bricklaying).
- The **weave technique** uses zigzag partings to divide base areas. It's effective for blending between perm rods with opposite base directions, and can also be used to create a smooth transition from the rolled areas into the unrolled areas of a partial perm.
- The **double-rod wrap** (AKA **piggyback wrap**) is for hair that's too long for each strand to be wrapped around a single rod. A strand of hair is wrapped on one rod from the scalp to the mid-point of the length (using the spiral technique), then the remainder of the hair strand is wrapped with another rod (using the croquignole technique). This technique doubles the number of rods used.

Chemical hair relaxers

Chemical hair relaxing rearranges the structure of curly hair into a smoother or straighter form, and the chemistry behind it is very similar to that of permanent waving: breaking the disulfide bonds during processing.

The two most common types of chemical hair relaxers are highly alkaline:

- **Ammonium thioglycolate (ATG or "thio")**, which is also used in permanent waving – although the thio used in hair relaxing is at a much higher concentration and pH (around 10) than in permanent waving. ATG is a type of no-lye relaxer – of which more later.

- **Hydroxide**, which is not used in permanent waving. The hydroxide ion is the active ingredient, which are very strong alkalis (pH over 13). As a result, the hair can swell up to twice its normal diameter.

Note: thio relaxer or thio permanent waves should NOT be applied to hair that's previously been treated with hydroxide: the hair won't properly relax or curl, and it may cause extreme damage.

How thio hair relaxing works

Thio (or ATG) hair relaxing produces soft, permanent curls. It is a milder method than hydroxide hair relaxing. The downside is a strong ammonia smell during the relaxing process. Here's how it works:

1. As with permanent waving, the alkaline pH in thio works to soften and swell the hair, while the thio itself breaks the disulfide bonds.
2. Once enough disulfide bonds are broken, the hair is straightened into its new shape.
3. The hair is rinsed of all relaxers and gently blotted.
4. **Neutralizer** is applied. As with permanent waving, the neutralization process rebuilds the disulfide bonds that were broken by the thio relaxer, through a process of oxidation. The neutralizer normally used is **hydrogen peroxide (H202)** – which is the same as the neutralizer used during thio waving). The neutralization process normally takes about 5–8 minutes to complete.

Note: if a client's hair has previously been treated with a hydroxide relaxer, you must not apply a thio relaxer or a thio permanent to the hair: it will not properly relax (or curl) the hair, and it may cause extreme damage.

How hydroxide hair relaxing works

Hydroxide is only used in hair relaxing – never permanent waving (whereas thio can be used for both). Here's how it works:

1: The **hydroxide ion** is the active ingredient, which is a very strong alkali (pH over 13). As a result, the hair can swell up to twice its normal diameter.

With thio relaxers, the pH of the thio softens/swells the hair, while the thio itself breaks the disulfide bonds. With hydroxide relaxers, the pH is so high (about 100,000,000 times more alkaline than the pH of hair) that the alkalinity alone breaks the bonds.

2: The disulfide bonds that are broken by hydroxide relaxers (through a process called **lanthionization**) are broken permanently. As a result, hair that's been treated with a hydroxide relaxer cannot then be permanently waved: the curl will not hold.

Whereas thio neutralization involves oxidation and rebuilding the disulfide bonds, hydroxide neutralization involves deactivating the alkaline residue left in the hair and lowering the pH of the hair and scalp. This is achieved by applying an acid-based shampoo (or normalizing lotion) to deactivate any remaining hydroxide ions – which lowers the pH of the hair and scalp. (As we know from earlier, acids neutralize alkalis.)

Any neutralizer that contains an oxidizing agent (such as those used for hair that's undergone thio relaxation) won't work, and will only damage the hair.

Types of hydroxide relaxers

Whereas there is just one type of thio relaxer, there are many types of hydroxide relaxer:

Lye relaxers

Lye relaxers can be thoroughly rinsed off without leaving any drying/damaging chemicals in the hair, meaning hair is usually healthier and stronger than no-lye relaxers. The problem, however, is that lye relaxers (otherwise known as caustic soda – also used in drain cleaners and hair depilatories) can cause scalp irritation.

There's one main type of lye relaxer: **sodium hydroxide (NaOH) relaxers** (pH 12.5–13.5). Sodium hydroxide relaxers are the oldest and most common type of chemical hair relaxer – and they're popular in salons because they work very quickly. They're effective for curly and extremely curly hair, although they may cause scalp irritation and damage the hair.

No-lye relaxers

No-lye relaxers generally aren't as hard on the scalp as lye relaxers, as the chemicals are milder. (Most relaxer kits made for home use are no-lye formulas.)

Unfortunately, they can sometimes cause dry/brittle hair because calcium hydroxide (CaOH) is often added to hydroxide relaxers – and the calcium can build up in the hair with repeated use. No-lye relaxers also take longer to process.

There are a few main types of no-lye relaxers:

Lithium hydroxide (liOH) and **potassium hydroxide (KOH) relaxers** (pH 12.5–13.5) have a chemistry (and performance) that's almost identical to lye relaxers, and hydroxide is still the active ingredient.

These no-lye relaxers are effective for curly and extremely curly hair, although they may cause scalp irritation and damage the hair.

Guanidine hydroxide relaxers (pH 13.0–13.5) also use hydroxide as their main ingredient. Unlike most other relaxers, however, guanidine hydroxide relaxers contain two components that must be mixed immediately before use.

Guanidine hydroxide relaxers are recommended for sensitive scalps and can be bought over the counter, but they can cause dry hair, as a result of a calcium build-up with repeated use. Their high pH means they swell the hair more than other hydroxide relaxers.

138

Ammonium sulfite and **ammonium bisulfate** (pH 6.5–8.5) are two types of **no-pH relaxer**. While they're "no-lye", they're not compatible with other hydroxide relaxers (but they *are* compatible with thio relaxers).

No-pH relaxers are intended for color-treated, damaged, or fine hair, and they won't completely straighten hair that's extremely curly.

… And remember that thio relaxers (which *aren't* a type of hydroxide relaxer) are also no-lye.

Base and no-base formulas

Hydroxide relaxers are usually sold in **base** and **no-base formulas**:

- **Base relaxers** need a **protective base cream** (AKA **protective base cream**) to be applied to the entire scalp before the application of the relaxer.

- **No-base relaxers** already contain a protective base cream that melts at body temperature, causing the cream to melt and settle onto the scalp in a thin protective coating as the relaxer is applied. (You should still apply a protective base cream to the entire hairline and around the ears, for added protection.)

Thio relaxer retouch: important things to remember

- Divide the hair into four sections.
- Make ¼ to ½ inch (0.6 to 1.25 centimeters) horizontal subsections, and apply the relaxer to the top of the strand.
- To avoid overprocessing or breakage, do not overlap the relaxer onto the previously relaxed hair.

- Only allow the relaxer to touch the scalp during the last few minutes of processing. The rest of the time, apply the relaxer as close to the scalp as possible, but don't touch the scalp itself with the product.

Hydroxide relaxer retouch: important thing to remember

- Apply a **protective base cream** to protect the entire scalp – especially on sensitive skin.
- Most manufacturers recommend applying a **protective cream/oil** to previously relaxed hair, in order to prevent overlapping. That is, it's important to relax the new growth only (to avoid damage).
- Many hair relaxing processes today include the application of a **normalizing conditioning lotion** after thoroughly rinsing the relaxer out of the hair. Normalizing conditioning lotions have an acidic pH that restores the hair pH before the final neutralizing shampoo.

Haircoloring

Identifying natural hair color

The most important step to becoming a good colorist is learning to identify a client's natural hair color.

A person's natural hair color is determined by the pigment found in the cortex (which is the middle layer of the hair). This pigment is called **melanin**. There are three types of melanin in the cortex:

- **Eumelanin** is responsible for black and brown colors to hair.
- **Pheomelanin** gives blond and red colors to hair.
- **Mixed melanin** is a combination of natural hair color that contains both eumelanin and pheomelanin.

Note: there is no such thing as "combination melanin". There is "mixed melanin", but no "combination melanin".

Color levels and tone

Hair color (whether natural or using hair color) is identified by a letter and a number – e.g. "6G" is level 6 (dark blond) with a gold (G) tone...

The number refers to the "level" – i.e. the lightness or darkness of a color. It's arranged on a scale of 1 (the darkest) to 10 (the lightest).

This **level system** is useful for determining the lightness or darkness of the client's natural hair color, but is also used by hair color manufacturers to standardize hair color charts and color bottles

/tubes. Some manufacturers go up to Level 12 rather than 10.

The letter is for the tone (AKA **hue**), which describes the warmth or coolness of a color). These tones can be described as warm, cool, or natural:

- **Warm tones** reflect more light, which means they can look lighter than their actual level. These tones are golden, orange, red, and yellow (sometimes referred to by manufacturers as auburn, amber, copper, strawberry, and bronze).
- **Cool tones** absorb more light, so they may look deeper than their actual level. These tones are blue, green, and violet (often referred to as smoky, drab, or ash).
- **Natural tones** are warm tones; they're often described as sandy or tan.

Base color is the predominant tone of a color. Select warm base colors to create brighter colors (such as red and gold tones). Select cool base colors for a more "ash" color result (which reveals less gold in the hair). Use a neutral color to soften and balance colors. (Neutral colors are often used to cover gray hair.)

Contributing pigment / undertone

Contributing pigment (AKA **undertone**) is the pigment that lies under the natural hair color, and it must be taken into consideration when choosing a hair color. When you lighten natural hair color, you expose contributing pigment. Haircoloring modifies this pigment to create new pigment.

The law of color

The law of color is a system for understanding color relationships. When combining colors, you will always get the same result from the same combination. For example:

- Equal parts of red and blue mixed together will always make violet.
- Equal parts of blue and yellow always make green.
- Equal parts of red and yellow always make orange.

The color wheel

The **color wheel** is an abstract illustration that organizes different colors around a circle. Its purpose is to explain visually the relationships between the three primary colors, the three secondary colors, and the six tertiary colors (for a total of 12 main colors).

Primary colors

The three **primary colors** are red, yellow, and blue. They are the "fundamental colors": all other colors are created from these three primaries.

- Blue is the strongest primary color, and it is the only "cool" primary color. **Blue can bring coolness, depth, or darkness to any color**.
- Red is the medium primary color. Adding red to blue-based colors will make them appear lighter, while adding red to yellow colors will make them appear darker.
- Yellow is the weakest primary color. When you add yellow to other colors, it will make them look lighter and brighter.

It's helpful to think of hair color in terms of different combinations of primary colors. For example, natural brown has the primary colors in the following proportions:

- Blue-B
- Red-RR
- Yellow-YYY

White can be used to lighten a color, and black can deepen a color.

Secondary colors

The three **secondary colors** are orange, green, and violet. Secondary colors are created by mixing equal parts of two primary colors:

- Green is an equal combination of blue and yellow.
- Orange is an equal combination of red and yellow.
- Violet is an equal combination of blue and red.

Tertiary colors

The six **tertiary colors** are "intermediate" colors – created by mixing a secondary color and its neighboring primary color on the color wheel in equal amounts. The tertiary colors are:

- Blue-green
- Blue-violet
- Red-violet
- Red-orange
- Yellow-orange
- Yellow-green

Hair color basics

Combining colors

Natural-looking hair color is made up of a combination of primary colors, secondary colors, and tertiary colors. When combined, the primary color is always the dominant color (e.g. when yellow and orange are combined, the new color is "yellow-orange" rather than "orange-yellow").

Complementary / neutralizing hair colors

Complementary colors are primary and secondary colors positioned directly opposite each other on the color wheel. E.g. red and green are complementary colors, as are yellow and violet.

Importantly, complementary colors can also correct/neutralize haircoloring errors (or unwanted natural tones in the client's hair):

- When hair is green, use red to balance (and vice-versa).
- When hair is blue, use orange to balance (and vice-versa).
- When hair is yellow, use violet to balance (and vice-versa).

SHOW COLOR WHEEL IMAGE AGAIN HERE

Note: on your exam, you may be asked which color "cancels", "neutralizes" or "tones out" another color. All these words mean the same thing! So if, for example, you're asked which color "neutralizes" yellow, the answer is violet. If you're asked which color "cancels" yellow, the answer is still violet.

- Warm skin tones look best when paired with a warm hair color. If your client wants to go blonde, a pinky blonde will therefore work best.
- Cool skin tones work well with cool hair colors.

The above "rules" have implications for makeup choice. E.g. if your client has blue eyes, you may think it's wise for her to use oranged-based eye makeup as the complementary choice. But if she has cool blue-black hair, the orange will not flatter. Instead, you should choose cool colors to coordinate with the hair color – such as red-violets, which are closest to orange on the color wheel but are still "cool".

Types of hair color

There are two main types of hair color:

<u>Non-oxidative</u> hair colors can be **temporary** or **semipermanent** (traditional).

<u>Oxidative</u> haircolors can be **demipermanent** (deposit only) or **permanent** (lift and deposit). These haircolors are mixed with hydrogen peroxide developers.

(A **hydrogen peroxide developer** is an oxidizing agent. There are many different types of **developer** (AKA **oxidizing agent** or **catalyst**), but hydrogen peroxide ($H2O2$) is the most commonly used in haircolor. All developers have a pH between 2.5 and 4.5.

When a developer is mixed with an oxidation haircolor, it supplies the necessary oxygen gas to develop the color molecules and create a change in natural hair color.

146

Volume measures the concentration and strength of hydrogen peroxide: the lower the volume, the less lift (lightening) achieved...

- 10 volume is usually for deposit-only.
- 20 volume is for the same level or one level of lift.
- 30 volume is for two levels of lift.
- 40 volume is for three to four levels of lift.

Note:
- All haircolors and lighteners except temporary require a **patch test** (AKA **predisposition test** or **allergy** test).
- Prior to coloring/lightening, all hair requires a **preliminary strand test** in order to determine the processing time, the condition of the hair after lightening, and the end results.
- Hydrogen peroxide must be stored in a cool, dark, dry place.

Temporary haircolor

- Will make only a physical change (not a chemical change) in the hair shaft.
- No patch test required.
- The color has large pigment molecules that do not penetrate the cuticle layer, which means only a coating of color is deposited – and it's easily removed by shampooing.
- Useful for those who wish to neutralize yellow hair or unwanted tones.
- Also useful for people who are allergic to aniline colors.
- Available as color rinses (applied weekly to shampooed hair), colored mousses and gels, hair mascara, spray-on haircolor, and color-enhancing shampoos.

Semipermanent haircolor

- Traditional semipermanent haircolor is a no-lift, deposit-only, non-oxidation haircolor.
- Not mixed with peroxide, which means it cannot lift/lighten color.
- Because it does not lighten hair, remember that color applied on top of existing color always creates a deeper color and alters the tone. (Therefore you may wish to select a color that's lighter than the desired shade.)
- Will last through several shampoos (depending on the hair's porosity) – usually 4–6 shampoos.
- The pigment molecules are small enough to partially penetrate the hair shaft and stain the cuticle layer, but they're also small enough to diffuse out of the hair during shampooing (which means the color will fade with each shampoo).
- Lasts four to six weeks.
- Although semipermanents are gentler than permanent haircolor, they contain some of the same dyes and require a patch test 24 to 48 hours before application.
- Toners are usually in this category of haircolor. (Toners are used on pre-lightened hair to achieve pale and delicate colors. Toners are also available as demipermanent haircolor products. Toners are discussed in more detail below.)

Demipermanent haircolor

- Demipermanent haircolor is a no-lift, deposit-only color.
- Usually mixed with a **low-volume developer** (AKA **oxidizing agent**).
- Decolorizing requires a high pH and a high concentration of peroxide, and demipermanents are lower pH and contain no peroxide. As a result, they cannot lighten/decolorize hair.

148

- Useful for introducing a client to a color service (because they create a change in tone without lightening the natural hair color).
- Good for blending/covering gray, or refreshing a faded permanent color on the mid-shaft and ends.
- Can also help to make color corrections and restore natural color.
- Requires a patch test 24 to 48 hours before application.

Permanent haircolor (often known as "single process tints")

- More alkaline than demipermanents, which means they can lighten and deposit (add) color at the same time and in a single process. They're also usually mixed with a **higher-volume developer** (AKA **oxidizing agent**).
- Used to match, lighten, and cover gray hair.
- Permanent haircolors contain uncolored dye precursors (called aniline derivatives), which are small, uncolored dyes that can easily penetrate into the hair shaft. These precursors combine with the hydrogen peroxide developers to form larger, permanent dye molecules that are then trapped within the cortex. As a result, they can't be easily shampooed out.
- As well as adding new colors to hair, permanent haircolors can also lighten (i.e. make a permanent change in) the natural hair color.
- Requires a patch test 24 to 48 hours before application.

Lighteners

- Chemical compounds that lighten hair by dispersing, dissolving, and decolorizing the natural hair pigment.
- They're used to create a light blond shade that can't be achieved with permanent haircolor alone. Can also be used to lighten the hair prior to the application of a final haircolor, lighten hair to a particular shade, brighten/lighten an existing

shade, lighten only certain parts of the hair, lighten dark natural or color-treated levels, lighten previously colored hair, and lighten hair without simultaneously depositing color.

- Lighteners are permanent.
- As with demipermanent and permanent haircolors, lighteners are mixed with **developers** (AKA **oxidizing agents**).
- To achieve a very light, pale blond, use a double-process application (AKA two-step coloring) – in which the hair is pre-lightened before the depositing color is applied:
    1. The lightening process involves using lightener on the hair for up to 90 minutes to achieve the desired lift/decolorization.
    2. The toning process involves adding soft tone back using toners.
- Hair will be damaged if you try to lift it past the "pale yellow" stage with lightener. To achieve a "baby-blond" look, you must instead lighten to a pale yellow and then neutralize the unwanted undertone (contributing pigment) with a toner.
- When conducting a lightener retouch, always lighten the new growth first. A cream lightener is generally used because it's less irritating to the scalp, and its consistency helps prevent overlapping of previously lightened hair. Overlapping can cause serious breakage (as well as lines of demarcation).
- The painting of lightener on clean, styled hair in a free-form technique is known as **balayage**.

Toners

- Toners are semipermanent or demipermanent haircolor products that involve no lift (i.e. they are deposit-only).

- They're mostly used to add character to blond hair after it's been lightened. They help to cancel out any brassy/unwanted tones, or to warm up blond hair.

How to color overly porous hair

Using fillers

Fillers are used to equalize porosity, which also helps to accomplish the following goals:

- Deposit color to faded ends and the hair shaft
- Help prepare the hair to hold a final color
- Prevent streaking and a dull appearance
- Prevent off-color results
- Produce more uniform, natural-looking color
- Produce uniform color when coloring pre-lightened hair back to its natural color

There are two types of fillers:

- Conditioner fillers
- Color fillers

Removing haircolor

It's sometimes necessary to remove some or all of the color from the hair in order to achieve the desired color. For example:

- The client may want to change to a lighter haircolor.
- The present color may have been a mistake.
- The color has built up/processed too dark due to a formulation error (happens occasionally).

To remove the haircolor, you will need to use a product known as a color or tint remover. This is a professional service that is only available in a salon.

Skin Care and Services

Hair removal

Permanent hair removal

The main permanent hair removal methods are:

- **Electrolysis** must be performed by a licensed electrologist.
- **Photoepilation** (AKA **intense pulsed light**, or **IPL**) can be by cosmetologists and estheticians in some states but not others.
- **Laser hair removal** can be performed by cosmetologists and estheticians in certain states, and requires specialist training.

Temporary hair removal

- **Shaving** is the most common – especially for men.
- **Tweezing** is often used to shape the eyebrows, and can also remove hairs from around the mouth and chin. The hair should be pulled in the direction of growth, and an acidic-based product should be used afterwards to close the pores.
- **Depilatories** are alkali substances that remove hair by dissolving it at the skin's surface.
- **Epilation** (such as **waxing**) is a temporary process, but the hairs will take longer to grow back (compared to other temporary methods) because the hair is removed from the bottom of the follicle. Hair should be at least ¼ inch (0.6 centimeters) long, in order to adhere to the wax.
- **Threading** (AKA **banding**) involves rolling a twisted piece of cotton thread along the surface of the skin. Hair is entwined in the thread and lifted from the follicle. It's practiced in many Eastern cultures and is becoming increasingly popular in the US.

- **Sugaring** uses a thick, sugar-based paste and produces the same results as wax – but with the added benefits that it can be used on sensitive skin, and the hair can be removed even if it's only ⅛ inch (0.3 centimeters) long.

Facials

The order of events for a basic facial is:

1. Drape.
2. Conduct a skin analysis.
3. Apply and remove cleanser.
4. Use steamer (if required) and extract comedones (if required).
5. Exfoliate (if client's skin is non-sensitive).
6. Choose a treatment cream, lotion, or massage cream appropriate for the skin type.
7. Massage the face, then remove the cream.
8. Use toner or freshener.
9. Apply a suitable mask, then remove the mask.
10. Apply toner, freshener, or astringent.
11. Apply moisturizer or sunscreen.
12. Remove draping.

Dry skin, oily skin, and acne-prone/problem skin will have slightly different steps and products. For example, electrotherapy and light therapy at certain stages to treat the skin.

Throughout the service, help your client relax by talking to them in a calm and professional manner.

Draping for a facial

Drape your client using a hair cap, headband, or towels. Ask your client to remove any jewelry. Note: unlike draping for hair services, you must use a protective hair cap or headband.

Determining skin type during skin analysis

Alipidic skin

Alipidic skin (AKA **dry skin**) doesn't produce enough sebum (indicated by an absence of visible pores). It becomes dehydrated (i.e. lacks moisture), and may look flaky or dry, with fine lines and wrinkles. It may also feel itchy or tight. It is treated by using hydrators that bind water to the skin's surface.

Oily skin

Oily skin produces too much sebum, and may be oily or greasy. The skin will have large pores, and these pores may be clogged from solidified sebum and dead cells building up in the hair follicle (known as **closed comedones** or **whiteheads**). These appear as small bumps just beneath the skin's surface.

Alternatively, the pores may contain **open comedones** (AKA **blackheads**), which are follicles impacted with solidified sebum and dead cell buildup.

Acne

The presence of pimples in oily areas indicates **acne** – which is considered a skin type because it is hereditary. With acne, follicles become clogged with sebum (as with comedones), but those follicles become infected due to the presence of acne bacteria. A buildup of bacteria in the follicle eventually causes the follicle to rupture, causing redness.

Acne pimples do not have a pus head. Pimples with a pus head are called pustules. Pus is fluid inside a pustule, made up of dead white blood cells that tried to fight the infection.

Hyperpigmentation

Hyperpigmentation (dark blotches of color) is usually caused by sun exposure or hormone imbalances. It can be treated with mild exfoliation and home care products that discourage pigmentation.

Sensitive skin

Sensitive skin will look "thin" and is easily inflamed by some skin care products. Avoid using strong cleansers, fragranced products, and strong exfoliants on sensitive skin.

Rosacea

Rosacea is considered a medical disorder (diagnosed by a dermatologist), and is characterized by redness, dilated blood vessels (telangiectasias), and distended capillaries (couperose).

Types of skin care products and treatments

Cleansers

Cleansers clean the surface of the skin and remove makeup. There are two main types: cleansing milks and foaming cleansers.

- Cleansing milks are lotions designed to remove makeup and cleanse dry and sensitive skin. They must be removed with a dampened facial sponge, soft cloth, or cotton pad.
- Foaming cleansers contain surfactants (detergents) that cause the product to foam and rinse off easily. They're generally for combination/oily skin, and they have varying

amounts of detergent ingredients to treat specific levels of oiliness.

Toners

Toners (AKA **fresheners** or **astringents**) are lotions that help to rebalance the pH, remove remnants of cleanser from the skin, and sometimes (with additional ingredients) hydrate, soothe, or exfoliate away dead skin cells. Fresheners and astringents are generally stronger, have a higher alcohol content, and treat oilier skin.

Exfoliants

Exfoliants remove excess dead skin cells from the skin's surface, helping it to look smoother and clearer. Exfoliants can also help clear the skin of clogged pores, and can improve the appearance of wrinkles, aging, and hyperpigmentation. There are two main types of exfoliant:

- **Mechanical exfoliants** physically remove dead cell buildup. E.g. gommages (AKA **roll-off masks**) are peeling creams that are rubbed off the skin, and microdermabrasion scrubs contain aluminum oxide crystals. (Microdermabrasion can also be used as a machine treatment. More on this later.)

- **Chemical exfoliants** contain chemicals that either loosen or dissolve dead cell buildup. Popular chemicals are alpha hydroxy acids (AHAs).

Microdermabrasion

Microdermabrasion is a type of mechanical exfoliation that involves shooting aluminum oxide crystals or other crystals at the skin with a hand-held device. The crystals bump off cells buildup in the skin, which is then vacuumed up by suction.

It is mainly used to treat surface wrinkles and aging skin, and it produces fast, visible results.

Peels

Peels are a type of chemical exfoliant, but they contain larger concentrations of AHA (20–30%) and are only available in salons. They will dissolve the surface cells of the skin to expose newer, fresher tissue.

Moisturizers

Moisturizers help to increase the moisture content of the skin's surface, and help to reduce the appearance of fine lines and wrinkles.

- Day protection products include **sunscreens** and **serums** (which penetrate the skin and treat various skin conditions).

Masks

Masks (AKA **masques**) are concentrated products that cleanse, exfoliate, tighten, tone, hydrate, and nourish the skin. There are many different types of mask:
- **Clay-based masks** are oil-absorbing cleansing masks that have an exfoliating and astringent effect on oily and combination skin, making large pores temporarily appear smaller.
- **Cream masks** contain oils and emollients as well as humectants. They aren't drying like clay masks are, and they're often used to moisturize.
- **Gel masks** can be used on sensitive or dehydrated skin, and they don't dry hard. They make the skin look more supple and hydrated.
- **Alginate masks** are often seaweed-based. They come in powder form and are mixed with water or serums. They must

160

be applied soon after mixing (usually over a treatment cream or serum), as they dry to form a rubberized texture. The masks form a seal that encourages the skin to absorb the treatment cream/serum underneath.

- **Paraffin wax masks** are melted slightly before use, and then they harden to a candle-like consistency after application. Like alginate masks, they are applied over a treatment cream to allow the cream to penetrate the skin more deeply. Eye pads and gauze are used over the eyes and facial hair because the mask is sticky.
- **Modelage masks** (AKA **modeling masks**) are also used with a treatment cream. They contain special crystals of gypsum (a plaster-like ingredient) and are mixed with cold water immediately before application – at which point the mixture changes consistency and hardens on the skin. A chemical reaction occurs that allows when the plaster and crystals mix with water to produce a gradual increase in temperature – which increases blood circulation and is beneficial for dry, mature skin or skin that looks dull and lifeless. As the mask is left on the skin, the temperature gradually cools.

Facial massage

Massage promotes absorption and relieves pain. Facial massage also helps to keep the facial skin healthy and the facial muscles firm.

The direction of movement is always from the insertion of the muscle toward its origin.

- The **insertion** is the portion of the muscle at the more movable attachment (where it is attached to another muscle or to a movable bone or joint).

- The **origin** is the portion of the muscle at the fixed attachment (to an immovable section of the skeleton).

Massaging a muscle in the wrong direction could lead to a loss of resiliency and sagging of the skin and muscles.

Basic massage manipulations

The following can all be performed on the face, but are applied to other parts of the body too.

To help your client relax, apply light but firm slow, rhythmic movements or very slow, light hand vibrations over the motor points for a short time. You could also pause briefly over the motor points, using light pressure.

- **Effleurage** is a light, continuous, rhythmic stroking movement with the fingers or palms, with no pressure used. It is very relaxing, and is the most common massage technique used during a manicure or pedicure (for both men and women), but is also used on the forehead, face, scalp, and other parts of the body. Effleurage warms up the muscles, so should be used at the start and end of all (stronger) massages.

- **Petrissage** involves kneading, squeezing, and pinching the tissues with a light, firm pressure. Although petrissage is typically used on larger surfaces (such as the arms and shoulders), you can also knead the cheeks using light pinching movements.

- **Friction** involves using fingers or palm to apply pressure to the skin using a deep rubbing movement, while moving over an underlying structure. It's typically used on the

162

scalp, arms, and hands. It has been known to benefit circulation and glandular activity of the skin. Chucking, rolling, and wringing are all variations of friction.

- **Tapotement** (AKA **percussion**) is the most stimulating type of massage, consisting of short, quick tapping, slapping, and hacking movements. It is usually done halfway through the massage. In facial massage, use only light tapping with the fingers.

- **Vibration** is a rapid shaking of the involved body part while the balls of the fingertips are pressed firmly on the point of application. It can be very relaxing, and should be performed toward the end of a massage.

Facial equipment and its uses

Many other products can enhance the facial treatment for clients:

- A **magnifying lamp** (AKA **loupe** or **mag light**) is a magnifying lens surrounded by a circular light, which provides a well-lit, enlarged view of the skin. It's useful for skin analysis as well as extraction of comedones, tweezing, electrolysis, and waxing – among other uses.

- A **facial steamer** heats and produces a stream of warm steam that can be focused on the client's face or other areas of skin. It helps to soften the tissues, which makes it more accepting of moisturizers and other treatment products. Steam also relaxes and softens comedones and clogged follicles, making them easier to extract. An **ozone steamer** creates an antibacterial effect on the skin.

- **Electrotherapy** uses electrical current to treat the skin. See the section on electrotherapy for more information.

- **Light-emitting diode (LED)** treatment uses concentrated light that flashes very rapidly, and it's used to minimize redness, warm lower-level tissues, stimulate blood flow, and improve skin smoothness. Red lights are used to treat aging and redness, while blue light is used on acne-prone skin.

- A **brushing machine** is used for mechanical exfoliation, and it is usually administered after or during a steam.

Facial makeup

Cosmetics for facial makeup

- **Foundation** (AKA **base makeup**) is used to cover or even out the coloring of the skin, and/or to conceal blemishes and other imperfections. It is usually the first cosmetic used during makeup application, although sometimes, a **color primer** is applied first to cancel out and help disguise skin discoloration.

    To choose the correct color, apply a small amount to the jawline; the color should match the skin on both the face and neck. (Your written exam may ask you which color to apply to very light or very dark skin, in an attempt to trick you. Don't fall for it! The answer is always that foundation should be the same as the natural skin tone.)

- **Concealer** is a thick, heavy type of foundation used to hide dark eye circles, dark splotches, and other imperfections.

- **Face powder** adds a matt or non-shiny finish to the face, and it absorbs excess oil and minimizes shiny skin. It is used to "set" the foundation, making it easier to apply other powder (such as blush).

- **Cheek color** (AKA **blush** or **rouge**) adds a natural-looking glow to the cheeks. Cream blush is used immediately after the foundation to blend color into the foundation, while powder blush is used after the foundation and powder have been applied. To create a natural look, you should apply cheek color no closer to the nose than the center of the eye.

- **Lip color** (AKA **lipstick** or **lip gloss**) changes or enhances natural lip color. The lip color must blend (not match) with the client's hair and eye color, as well as with other makeup used. It should never be applied directly from the container unless it belongs to the client. Instead, it must be applied with a one-application disposable lip brush (or removed from the container with a spatula and placed on a palette).

- **Lip liner** is used to outline the lips and to keep the lipstick from bleeding into small lines around the mouth.

- **Eye shadow** accentuates or contours the eyelids. **If your client has close-set eyes,** lightly apply shadow upward from the outer edge of the eyes.

- **Eyeliner** is applied close to the lashes. It makes the eyes appear larger and the lashes appear fuller.

- **Eyebrow pencil** (AKA **eyebrow shadow**) is used to darken the eyebrows, correct their shape, or fill in sparse areas.

- **Brow powder** is applied to the brows with a brush. It clings to eyebrow hairs, making the brows appear darker and fuller.

- **Mascara** darkens, defines, and thickens the eyelashes. When applying, always use a disposable wand dipped inside a clean tube of mascara.

Nail Care and Services

Nail structure

Nail anatomy

- The **nail plate** is a hardened keratin plate that sits on and covers the nail bed. It is more porous than normal skin of an equal thickness, and water can pass through it. As it grows, the nail plate slowly slides across the nail bed.

  It appears to be one solid piece, but is actually constructed of about 100 layers of nail plate cells (which are created by matrix cells).

- The **free edge** is the part of the nail plate that extends over the tip of the finger or toe.

- The **nail bed** is found just underneath the nail plate. It has a rich supply of blood vessels, which gives it a pinkish appearance from the lunula to the area just before the free edge.

- The **matrix** is where the nail plate cells are formed, and it is composed of matrix cells. The matrix area contains nerves, lymph, and blood vessels to nourish the matrix cells.

- The visible part of the matrix is called the **lunula**: it's the whitish, half-moon shape underneath the base of the nail. Every nail has a lunula, but some are short and are hidden under the eponychium. In tests, it's sometimes referred to as the extension of the cuticle over the half-moon at the base.

- The **cuticle** is the dead, colorless tissue that has pulled from the eponychium and attached to the nail plate. Its job is to seal the space between the nail plate and the eponychium to help prevent injury and infection.

  Note: products marketed as nail cuticle moisturizers, softeners, or conditioners aren't actually for the cuticle (which is dead skin). These products are actually for the eponychium, lateral sidewalls, and hyponychium – not the cuticle.

  Cuticle removers *do* remove the dead cuticle: they quickly dissolve soft tissue.

- The **eponychium** is the living skin at the base of the nail plate that covers the matrix area. It can be hard to tell the difference between the nail cuticle and the eponychium.

  Cosmetologists are allowed to gently push back the eponychium, but are prohibited from cutting or trimming it, since it is living skin.

- The **perionychium** is the living skin that borders the root and sides of a fingernail or toenail.

- The **hyponychium** lies between the fingertip and the free edge. It is a slightly thickened layer of skin that forms a protective barrier to prevent infection.

- **Specialized ligaments** attach the nail bed and matrix bed to the underlying bone.

- The **nail folds** are folds of normal skin surrounding the nail plate, which form the nail groove (i.e. the furrow) on each side of the nail. The **sidewall** (AKA the **lateral nail fold**) is the fold of skin overlapping the side of the nail.

Nail growth

- The average rate of nail plate growth in a normal adult is about 1/10 inch to 1/8 inch (2.5 mm to 3 mm) per month.

- Children's nails grow more rapidly, while elderly people's nails grow at a slower rate.

- Nails grow faster in summer than in winter.

- Nail growth rates dramatically increase during the last trimester of pregnancy, then decreases quickly back to normal after the baby has been born (due to changes in hormone levels).

- Nail growth is fastest on the middle finger nail and slowest on the thumb, and toenails grow more slowly than fingernails.

- Although toenail plates grow more slowly, they're ticker because the toenail matrix is longer than the fingernail matrix.

Manicuring

Equipment vs implements vs materials

- **"Equipment"** refers to ALL nail tools that are NOT "implements" – such as manicure tables, containers, and chairs.

- **"Implements"** are the tools that are used to perform nail services. There are "single use"/"disposable" implements (such as various product application brushes) and "multiuse"/"reusable" (such as metal pushes and tweezers).

- **"Materials"** (or "supplies") are meant to be single-use only. They include gloves, dust masks, single-use/terry cloth towels, gauze, cotton balls, plastic-backed pads, and abrasive nail files and buffers.

Health, safety, and hygiene

It is important to note the following information for your exam:

- Cosmetologists are particularly prone to hypersensitivity reactions from various chemicals. To avoid this, the **Occupational Safety and Health Administration (OSHA)** requires salon ventilation where chemical services are performed – as well as proper personal protective equipment (PPE).

- **Gloves** are an example of PPE. Since chemicals can be absorbed through the skin, OSHA recommends nitrile gloves: they protect against chemicals where latex and vinyl do not, helping to prevent dermatitis.

According to OSHA, gloves are also the most important way to protect cosmetologists from exposure to microbes during service.

- **Spray disinfectant** is a product capable of destroying fungi, virus, bacteria, and bacterial spores on a non-porous surface.

- **Soap** must be used to disinfect and clean your hands and the client's hands before a service begins. Soap removes over 90% of pathogenic microbes from the hands. Liquid soaps are preferred because bar soaps harbor bacteria.

- A **gauze and cotton wipe container** is required to hold absorbent cotton, lint-free wipes, or gauze squares. It must have a lid to protect the contents from dust and contaminants.

- A **disinfection container** must also be used. It must be large enough to completely immerse several service sets – i.e. sets of all the tools that will be used in a service.

The basic nail service

A basic professional nail services include three different, solvent-based products, applied one layer at a time, to the nails:

- The **base coat** creates a colorless layer on the natural nail (and/or nail enhancement), and it helps the polish to adhere to the nail. It also helps to prevent the polish pigments from staining the nail plate.

  Like nail polishes, base coats contain solvents designed to evaporate. After evaporation, a sticky film remains on the nail's surface to increase adhesion of the colored polish.

- The **polish** (AKA **enamel, lacquer,** or **varnish**) is a solvent-based colored film that adds color or special visual effects (such as sparkles). It is usually applied in two coats over the base coat.

- The **top coat** is applied over the polish to prevent chipping and to add shine. It contains ingredients that creates a hard, shiny film after the solvent has evaporated.

Other nail services/products

- **Nail creams**, **lotions**, and **oils** soften dry skin around the nail plate and increase the flexibility of natural nails.

- **Cuticle remover** loosens and dissolves dead tissue on the nail plate so that it can be removed. Avoid skin contact as much as possible, as it will lead to dryness. Always apply from a clean, sterile palette – ideally using a cotton-tipped wooden stick.

- **Nail bleach** removes discoloration or stains on the nail plate.

- **Gel polish** is a form of nail color that lasts 10 to 21 days, and it avoids the constant smudging that clients experience after a regular manicure. The application is similar to traditional polishes (but not identical).

- **Nail hardener** improves the surface hardness/durability of weak or thin nail plates. It can be applied before the base coat or after as a top coat (depending on the manufacturer's recommendations).

- **Nail polish accelerators** are applied over a top coat to hasten the drying of nail polishes. They're usually applied with a dropper, a brush, or are sprayed onto the surface of the polish. They work by pulling solvents from the nail polish, causing the colored film to form more quickly.

- **Hand creams** and **lotions** add a finishing touch to a manicure, making the skin and manicure look as beautiful as possible.

- **Nail conditioner** reduces brittleness of the nail and dry cuticles. It is often applied at night before bed.

Implements

Multi-use implements

- **Metal pushers** (often incorrectly called cuticle pushers) gently scrape cuticle tissue from the nail plate.

- **Nail nippers** are used to trim away dead skin from around the nails.

- **Tweezers** can lift small bits of debris from the nail plate, retrieve and place nail art, remove implements from disinfectant solutions, and much more.

- **Nail clippers** shorten the free edge quickly.

- **Brushes and applicators** must be cleaned and disinfected before use on another client. If they can't be properly cleaned and disinfected, they must be disposed off after a single use. (Except nail polish brushes, because they're stored in an oxygen-free, water-free liquid, which doesn't allow for the growth of microbes.)

- **Wooden pushers** remove cuticle tissue from the nail plate (by gently pushing). They can also be used to clean under the free edge of the nail. Additionally, pushers can be used to apply products. They're not intended for reuse.

- **Nail brushes** are plastic with nylon brushes, and can be used in many ways – including (importantly) to scrub implements clean before disinfection.

Abrasive nail files and buffers (generally considered single-use "materials")

These are available in many different types and grits (from less than 180 grits per centimeter to over 240).

The lower the grit, the larger the abrasive particles on the file and the more aggressive its action. Therefore…

- Lower-grit abrasives (less than 180 grit) are aggressive and will quickly reduce the thickness of a nail surface. They also produce deeper and more visible scratches. They're not generally used on natural nails, as they can cause damage.
- Medium-grit abrasives (150 to 180 grit) are used to smooth and refine surfaces. The 180-grit is used to shorten and shape natural nails (the free edge).

- Fine-grit abrasives (240 grit and higher) are for buffing, polishing, and removing fine scratches.

Some abrasive boards/buffers can be cleaned and disinfected, but most must be thrown away after one use.

Two-way or three-way buffers (AKA **shiners**) **are commonplace these days, and they have tended to replace the chamois in salons for creating a beautiful shine on nails**. When creating a high shine, begin with the lowest grit abrasive surface, move to the higher grit, and then finish with the shining surface, which tends to have no grit.

ANSWER:

What implement adds shine and smooths wavy ridges on the natural nail during a manicure?

Course file

Nail buffer

Nail brush

Metal file

Basic nail shapes for women
- A **square** nail is completely straight across the free edge, with no rounding at the outside edges.

- A **squoval** nail has a square free edge that is rounded off at the corner edges. If the nail extends only slightly past the fingertip, this shape is particularly sturdy – because there's no square edge to break off. Clients who work with their hands (nurses, computer technicians, office workers, landscapers, etc.) will benefit from having shorter, squoval nails.

- A **round** nail is slightly tapered, and it should extend just a bit past the fingertip. This is the most common nail shape for male clients.

- An **oval** nail is similar to the squoval but with even more rounded corners (and often longer). It's considered a classic, conservative nail shape that's flattering to most people's hands – and it's often preferred by clients who have their hands on display a lot (businesspeople, teachers, salespeople, etc.).

- A **pointed** nail is suitable for thin hands with long fingers and narrow nail beds. The nail is tapered and longer than usual – and it's weaker and more likely to break. This nail shape is usually found on enhancements rather than natural nails.

Pedicuring

Pedicure-specific implements

- **Curettes** have a small, scoop-shaped end that allows for more efficient removal of debris from the nail folds, eponychium, and hyponychium areas.
- **Nail rasps** have a grooved edge for filing and smoothing the edges of the nail plate. They help to reduce the sides of the free edge that might grow into the tissues and potentially cause an ingrown toenail.
- **Pedicure nail files** may be metal when used on toenails. Use a medium grit file for shaping, and a fine grit file for finishing and sealing the edges.
- **Large foot files** (AKA **pedicure paddles**) reduce and smooth calluses to create softer skin.

Other products that are specific to pedicures

Pedicuring products include all those used in manicuring, plus some others:

- **Soaks** soften and cleanse the skin. The soak sets the stage for the rest of the pedicure.
- **Exfoliating scrubs** remove dry, flaky skin and reduce calluses. Note: many products help to reduce calluses. Others include scribs, callus softeners, pedicure paddles, and large foot files.
- **Masks** cleanse, exfoliate, tighten, tone, hydrate, and nourish the skin.

- **Pedicure lotions and creams** help to condition and moisturize the skin of the legs and feet, soften calluses, and provide slip for massage.
- **Callus softeners** soften and smooth thickened tissue (calluses). After the product softens the callus, it is more easily reduced and smoothed with files or paddles. Safety glasses should be worn whenever using them, as they are potent liquid formulas.

Nail enhancements

Nail enhancements are formed by combining three basic ingredients: monomer liquid, polymer powder, and a catalyst to speed up the hardening process.

"Mono" means one and "mer" means units, so a monomer is one unit – called a molecule. "Poly" means many, so "polymer" means a substance formed by combining many small molecules (monomers) into very long, chain-like structures.

Nail enhancements (AKA **acrylics** or **sculptured nails**) are part of the acrylic family.

Monomer liquids and polymer powders come in many colors, which can be used alone or blended in four basic ways:

- Over the natural nail (as a protective overlay)
- Over a nail tip
- On a form to create a nail extension
- To create small works of art on top or inside a nail enhancement

Supplies required for monomer liquid and polymer powder nail enhancements

You will need:

Monomer liquid

Monomer liquid – which will be combined with polymer powder to form the nail enhancement. The mix ratio of these products should be one-and-a-half times more liquid than powder – which will produce a "medium bead", which is smooth, round, and shiny.

Polymer powder

Polymer powder is available in white, clear, pink, and many other colors. The color(s) you choose will depend on which nail enhancement method you're using.

When not in use, the liquid and powder must be stored in covered containers. Before use, they are each poured into a special container called a **dappen dish**, which have narrow openings to minimize evaporation of the liquid into the air.

Application brushes

Application brushes are usually made of natural kolinsky, sable, or a blend of both. (Synthetic or less expensive brushes don't' pick up enough liquid or release it properly.) The brushes are oval, round, or square, and they come in a variety of sizes. The most popular brush (for both the monomer and polymer) is the **#8 oval brush**.

Nail dehydrator

Nail dehydrator is applied to the natural plate only (avoid skin contact). It removes surface moisture/oil, and prevents the nail enhancement from "lifting" before primer has been applied.

Nail primer

Nail primer is used after the nail dehydrator to help the enhancement adhere to the nail. One end of the primer molecule chemically bonds to the nail protein in the natural nail, while the other end bonds to the monomer liquid in the nail enhancement.

Primer can be acid-based or non-acid/acid-free. Acid-based primer is corrosive to the skin and potentially dangerous to the eyes. Acid-free primers work just as well (perhaps better), but aren't corrosive. Even so, skin contact should be avoided during application.

Note: primer can *also* be used to reduce the "mix ratio", reduce surface moisture on the nail (like a nail dehydrator does), and remove oil (also like a nail dehydrator does). **Its main function, however, is to improve adhesion**.

Abrasives

"Abrasives" is used to describe nail files (plastic or wood) and buffers (plastic and sponge).

All abrasives have a grit number: the lower the number, the rougher the abrasive will be (although the material used will also play a part – e.g. sponge will be gentler). Here are the most common abrasives used:

- To thin out an enhancement product for a refill or rebalance, **you'll need a coarse-grit abrasive (100 grit or**

lower). Avoid using anything lower (i.e. more abrasive), as it can damage the soft, freshly created enhancement.

- **A medium-grit abrasive (150 to 180 grit)** is used for initial shaping of the nail perimeter, refining the surface shape of a nail enhancement, or smoothing the surface before buffing.

- For finish filing, refining, and buffing (as well as for shaping the free edge of the natural nail), a **fine-grit abrasive (240 grit or higher)** is used.

- To create a high shine on a natural nail or enhancement where no polish will be worn, use a **shiner**. **A shiner is a buffer with three sides (usually 400, 1,000, and 4,000 grit)**, and you must buff the entire nail with the lowest-grit side first and then repeat with the other sides. Shiners can sometimes have just two sides – and with these, you may like to start with a 240- or 350-grit buffer before using the shiner.

To extend the length of the nail first...

Nail forms

Nail forms are placed under the free edge of the nail, and they're used as a foundation on which to create nail enhancements that are longer than the natural nail.

Single-use (disposable) nail forms are made of paper or Mylar and coated with adhesive backs. Multiuse (reusable) nail forms are made of pre-shaped plastic or aluminum.

Nail tips extend the length of the nail in a different way. These are available in a wide variety of shapes and colors, and they're adhered to the tip of the natural nail with a nail adhesive. (The thickest nail adhesive is gel-like and referred to as a "resin".)

Nail tips aren't strong enough to wear on their own, so they must be overlaid with an enhancement product too.

Some nail tips fully cover the entire nail plate.

- Safety products include **safety eyewear**, **dust masks**, and **protective gloves** (usually made of nitrile polymer powder).

- To remove these nails, apply a solvent and push them off.

Light cured gels

When a UV gel resin is exposed to UV or LED light (depending on the gel), a chemical inside the gel (called a "photoinitiator") initiates a reaction that causes the gel to harden/"cure".

Light cured gels are easy to apply, file, and maintain – and they have almost no odor. Although they're not as hard as monomer liquid/polymer powder enhancements, they're more flexible.

You're Done!

Congratulations on finishing *Cosmetology Guru: The Essential Information You Need to Pass the First Time (and Nothing Else!)*.

Do you want to cement your knowledge and make sure you *really* understand it? Do you wish to feel reassured that you can recall that knowledge under exam conditions – with the types of questions that will appear on the real thing?

Then look no further than **Cosmetology Guru Online** – the perfect complement to this book. **Cosmetology Guru Online** contains hundreds of practice questions PLUS six simulated exams (which replicate the real-life exams you'll be taking).

When you buy **Cosmetology Guru Online**, you'll get:

- **Hundreds of practice questions**

- **Six simulated exams**

- **A condensed version of this book** – so you can learn on your device whenever you have a spare moment

Cosmetology Guru Online is compatible with computers, smartphones, and tablets, so you can access it whichever way you please.

Visit www.cosmetologyguru.com and enter 30OFFNOW at checkout for 30% off.

If you have any questions or concerns before you buy, simply email contact@cosmetologyguru.com and we'll get back to you right away!

Good luck in your exam, and please do let us know how you do: contact us at contact@cosmetologyguru.com and share your success story!

The Cosmetology Guru Team

Made in the USA
Middletown, DE
15 November 2024

64669182R00106